*Just incase decide to
a visit, th
you need to know*

mads xx

SYDNEY

ULRIKE LEMMIN-WOOLFREY

Contents

Sydney 5
Planning Your Time 9
Orientation 10

Sights 11
The Rocks and Circular Quay 11
Central Business District (CBD) 18
Darling Harbour and Haymarket 27
Kings Cross 32
Paddington 35
The Northern Shore 37
Island Hopping in Sydney Harbour 40
The Beaches 41
Day Tours 44

Sports and Recreation 47
Gardens and Parks 47
Biking 47
Hiking 50
Snorkeling and Diving 50
Surfing 50
Kayaking 51
Sailing 52
Cruises and Rides 52
Whale-Watching 54
Spectator Sports 54

Entertainment and Events 56
Nightlife 56
The Arts 60
Festivals and Events 61

Shopping 65
Shopping Districts and
   Shopping Centers 65
Clothing and Accessories 65
Gifts 67
Antiques and Curios 68
Books 68

Accommodations 69
The Rocks and Circular Quay 69
Central Business District (CBD) 71
Darling Harbour and Haymarket 73
Kings Cross and Darlinghurst 75
Paddington 76
The Northern Shore 76
The Beaches 77

Food 79
The Rocks and Circular Quay 79
Central Business District (CBD) 81
Darling Harbour and Haymarket 82
Kings Cross 83
Paddington 84
The Northern Shore 85
The Beaches 86

Information and Services 87
Tourist Information 87
Hospitals, Emergency Services,
   and Pharmacies 87

Money 87
Postal Services 88
Internet and Telephone 88

Getting Around 88
Getting to and from the Airport 88
Public Transport 88
Taxis 89
Driving 89

Blue Mountains 90
Sights 90
Recreation 94
Accommodations 94

Food 95
Information and Services 95
Getting There and Around 96

Hunter Valley 97
Wineries 98
Recreation 99
Accommodations 100
Food 101
Information and Services 101
Getting There and Around 101

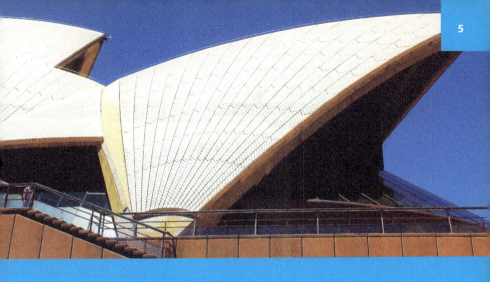

Sydney

Highlights

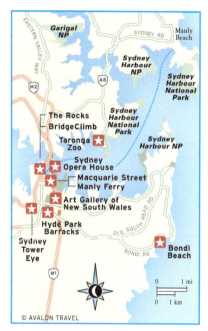

★ **The Rocks:** This is where it all started, where the First Fleet landed and the first settlers arrived, voluntarily or not. There is a great atmosphere of history in the air, the buildings are all wonderful, and the area is dotted with cafés, restaurants, and shops (page 11).

★ **Sydney Opera House:** It really doesn't get more iconic than the Sydney Opera House, one of the most widely recognized buildings in the world (page 11).

★ **BridgeClimb:** To get a view like no other, climb Sydney Harbour's iconic "coat hanger" bridge. It looks steeper than it is and the climb is slow with plenty of breaks, making it accessible for nearly everybody (page 15).

★ **Manly Ferry:** This commuter ferry goes past the opera house, all along the harbor, and past the islands to the entrance to the ocean at Manly. For a handful of dollars you get hundreds of dollars worth of views (page 18).

★ **Macquarie Street:** If you just see one street in Sydney, this must be it. Every building is historic, and the road stretches from the opera house, past the Royal Botanic Gardens, to Hyde Park. Take your time and pop into all the buildings along the way, and you'll have a great idea of Australia's history (page 21).

★ **Hyde Park Barracks:** This museum concentrates on Australia's first settlers, the workers that built the colony—how they lived, worked, struggled (page 22).

★ **Art Gallery of New South Wales:** Located in the beautiful Domain, with great views, the gallery is a fantastic collection of old European, contemporary, indigenous, and ancient Asian art (page 23).

★ **Sydney Tower Eye:** Get a good overview of this sprawling metropolis from up high. You can even do yoga or be daring and do a skywalk (page 26).

★ **Taronga Zoo:** Sydney is all about views—even the zoo has them. Stand by the giraffes and see the Sydney skyline, opera house, and bridge from there. Oh, and the animals, from near and far, are wonderful, too (page 37).

★ **Bondi Beach:** This is one of the best-known beaches on the globe. Curved along the bay, fringed by rocky outcrops and the "village," as the suburb proudly calls itself, the beach attracts surfers, bathers, and the famous lifeguards. And the stunning Bondi to Coogee walk starts here (page 41).

To call Sydney iconic is an understatement. The poster city for Australia is all about the harbor, with its natural beauty as well as the Sydney Opera House and the Sydney Harbour Bridge. One of the largest and most beautiful natural harbors in the world, the setting could not be more glorious if an entire conglomerate of top-notch town planners had tried.

Sydney's ancient history goes back to some 50,000 years ago, when anthropologists believe the Aboriginal people first reached Sydney's natural harbor, yet its more modern history does not start until 1770, when Captain James Cook landed at Botany Bay just south of Sydney and brought his tales of the long-sought and finally found Great Southern Land back to Britain. A few years later, with the American Revolution hampering the habit of transporting convicts from Britain to the Americas, it was decided that the land around Botany Bay would be suitable for future convict deportation. When the First Fleet of 11 ships landed on the southern coast, Captain Arthur Phillip deemed Botany Bay unsuitable due to its lack of fresh water, but he discovered a near perfect natural harbor a little farther up the coast, eventually deciding to settle at Sydney Cove, now Circular Bay.

Sydney Cove, and with it Sydney itself, was named after Captain Phillip's superior, Lord Sydney, and the day of the arrival of the First Fleet, on January 26, 1788, has gone down in history as the annually celebrated Australia Day. The first settlers were not terribly well chosen to establish a new colony in the land down under, with no carpenters, smiths, or even farmers among the officers or the convicts, but inroads were made due to teamwork, the need to survive, and sheer determination.

More and more voluntary settlers arrived together with regular supply ships from the homeland, trade routes were established with the Americas and Asia, and the wealth of the new world began to show in imposing buildings commissioned by Governor Lachlan Macquarie (governor of New South Wales from 1810 to 1821). The discovery of gold

Previous: Sydney Opera House; Sydney's Central Business District. **Above:** one of Paddington's little cafés.

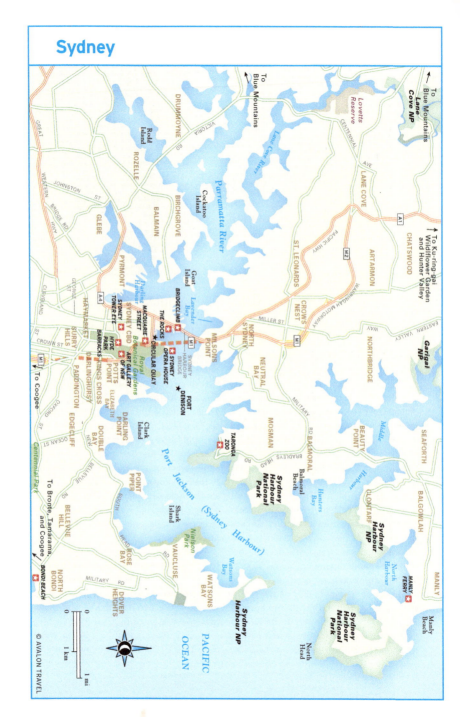

in the mid-1800s further drew more settlers and established the wealth and grandeur of Sydney.

Today, Australia's largest city has nearly five million inhabitants. Sydney spreads itself sumptuously along its sunken river valley, hemmed by some of the world's most expensive real estate. Being the financial capital of the country, the first stop for most visitors and would-be immigrants, the media hub, and the entrepreneurial engine of the entire continent, Sydney not only attracts money, it also demands it. Just recently, Sydney was named one of the most expensive cities of the world to live in.

Pricey or not, people come to Sydney and fall in love. The beauty of the harbor, the majestic buildings in the town center (Central Business District or CBD) harking back to prosperous times that started back in the early 1800s, and the proximity of some of the world's most famous and surfable beaches along the Pacific coast, together with the city being the hub from where to reach the rest of this rather large country, all make for a popular gateway to Australia and a stunning city in its own right.

More than a third of Sydney's population was born outside Australia, and most Australians descend from immigrants themselves, so the feeling in the city is one of a worldly cosmopolitan metropolis—a metropolis where at every turn you hear a different language, can enjoy a vast array of cuisines, and have great shopping. Still it is a very historic city, even if this is a relative term when you think how young the modern history of Australia is. Just as in Manhattan, it pays to look up and marvel at the variety of architecture: You have the imposing Victorian buildings, majestic Art Deco towers, and stunning modern high-rises.

Sydney is a great mixing and melting pot of people and styles. It is stunning and mostly sunny, offering beaches, pavements, history, and modernity. It captivates you. And often doesn't let you go again, as most of the recent immigrants to this Lucky Country can pay testament to.

PLANNING YOUR TIME

Like all of the world's great cities, Sydney is brimming with things to see and do, and demands time. With nearly five million people calling Sydney home, it is not only Australia's largest city, but also larger than the inner city of Los Angeles, and even if you would move here, you'd never get to see everything or experience it all. So you will just have to try to squeeze as much into your allocated time as possible. And it all depends on what your interests are.

If you are a history buff, numerous very good museums and heritage buildings could keep you busy, but you can get a good idea of Sydney's and Australia's history within a couple of days, taking in the main museums and sights, such as the Hyde Park Barracks, Macquarie Street, and The Rocks.

If you are a pleasure seeker, seek no further and head for the harbor and the beaches, then off into the city for some bar-hopping, excellent food, and great shopping. Depending on whether you want to learn to surf from scratch or if you are in need of a deep tan, then several days will be needed.

But most likely you are in Sydney because you have finally come to see the great continent down under and, while not the capital, Sydney is still *the* city to see when in Australia, and you will want to get a good idea of what it's all about, get a basic understanding of the history, see the iconic landmarks, and either see or sample Bondi Beach. In that case you should allocate around three days.

The handy thing in Sydney is the public transport. Yes, ask any local and they are likely to moan, but visitors can get a MyMulti card for either a day or a week (the weekly pass is worth it if you use it for more than two days) and literally hop on and off any bus, train, or ferry within the city limits and get everywhere easily. Download the public transport app on your phone. You can type in where you wish to go and it will tell you exactly how to get there with type of transport, directions if you will have to walk some, and time allowances.

And most likely you won't have to worry

about the weather too much. Sydney does have seasons, but depending on where you are from, even the winter (July-August) is still a lot more pleasant than in the rest of the world. According to the Australian Bureau of Meteorology, Sydney has, on average, seven hours of sunshine a day. Its temperature ranges from an average winter minimum of 9 and a maximum of 17 degrees Celsius to a peak summer maximum average of 26 degrees. Sydney's rainfall averages 1,213 millimeters a year, with an average of 11 wet days per month. More than 40 percent of this rain falls between March and June. But if you want to play it safe, then spring or fall are the best months, when it's not too hot to walk along the city's pavements and not so cold that you can't sit outside and enjoy the views. Spring generally has a little less rainfall than fall, but both have perfect temperatures for exploring.

Sydney does not have any great fluctuations in visitor numbers over the year, but bear in mind that the country's school summer holidays are across Christmas and New Year, so that is a bit of a hot spot. That said, there is no better place to be over New Year's Eve than Sydney, as long as you can cope with the crowds and the inflated prices. But that's only for a couple of nights and then it gets back to its normal—if pricey—self.

ORIENTATION

It is obvious from maps and just being there that Sydney is dominated by its harbor, which effectively splits the city in two. It's in a coastal basin, with the borders being the Pacific Ocean and its lovely Manly and Bondi beaches on either side of the harbor entrance to the east, and the formerly separate settlement of Parramatta being slowly swallowed up on the west side farther inland, where the broad harbor narrows into the mangrove-lined Parramatta River. On the northern side the sprawl continues through increasingly green suburbs up to the Hawkesbury River, while Botany Bay provides a natural border in the south.

The city's center, or **CBD,** with its towering skyscrapers and large colonial buildings, sits on the south side of the harbor and stretches from the busy ferry port of Circular Quay down to the railway hub of Central Station, bordering the chic residential areas of Woolloomooloo and Darlinghurst on the east and Darling Harbour on the west.

Sydney is quite hilly, increasingly so in the west toward the Blue Mountains, which can reach up to 1,215 meters (3,986 feet) above sea level. The hills allow tantalizing glimpses of water in the distance, even from the inner city suburbs, which adds to the attraction of most of Sydney's residential areas.

Sydney has some easy connections with major highways reaching out into the various suburbs: the **Pacific Highway** connects the CBD across **Sydney Harbour Bridge** with the north, indeed all the way to Brisbane and beyond. There is a toll fare charged when crossing Sydney Harbour Bridge southbound only, and the same system works for the Sydney Harbour Tunnel, with tolls charged each time. Once on the north side, **Military Road** gets you to most suburbs along the way to Manly.

Southbound, the **Southern Cross Drive** connects easiest to the airport, while **Parramatta Road** is a fast westward stretch to Parramatta past the docks and Sydney Olympic Park. Toward the east, **Oxford Street** winds itself through the suburbs; it's not fast, but it hits all the main suburbs along the way to Bondi Beach and is the route of choice for the buses, too.

Once you are heading out of the sprawling city limits, you may well encounter further **toll roads,** including the Eastern Distributor, which is only charged northbound, as well as the M5 East Freeway, the M5 South-West Motorway, the Westlink M7, the Hills M2 Motorway, and both the Lane Cove Tunnel and the Cross City Tunnel, which are all charged in each direction.

Sights

THE ROCKS AND CIRCULAR QUAY
★ The Rocks

The Rocks, on the west side of Circular Quay, the former Sydney Cove, is where Sydney began; indeed, where Australia began its modern history. The small lanes, cobbled streets, and historic buildings hark back to a time when this was not the atmospheric and friendly place it is now. The Rocks has a dark and sinister past, where rum was the currency, crime and prostitution were on the daily menu, and the living was not easy. This is where the first settlers, mostly convicts who had achieved their freedom, lived in ramshackle terraced houses (some still to be seen at Susannah Place Museum) and went out across the fast growing city to help build the soon to be magnificent and rich Sydney.

Today, apart from pretty much every building having a historic value, The Rocks nestle underneath the pylons of the grand bridge, and many tours, anything from ghost tours to pub crawls, tell their own story of this area, which started up around little Campbell's Cove, where you can now catch a tall ship to cruise the harbor and get a little bit of the feeling that the first settlers might have felt—just imagine the city without any buildings and houses, without the opera house and the bridge, just green bushland growing across the undulating hills. It must have been quite a sight.

The Rocks should really be your starting point, as it was then, but you may find it difficult to resist the lure of the Sydney Opera House. So start there, walk along Circular Quay, exhaust your memory card in your camera, and head to The Rocks. Soak up the atmosphere, get a feel for the history, imagine what it was like. Pop into one of the many cafés, have lunch, go out in the evening, and sit out on the pavement with a drink. Then move on to the rest of Sydney.

★ Sydney Opera House

The one building everybody associates with Australia, the **Sydney Opera House** (Bennelong Point, tel. 02/9250-7250, www.sydneyoperahouse.com, daily 9am-5pm, tours adult $35, child $24.50, family $90), was inscribed in the World Heritage List in June 2007 with the comments: "Sydney Opera House is a great architectural work of the 20th century. It represents multiple strands of creativity, both in architectural form and structural design, a great urban sculpture carefully set in a remarkable waterscape and a world-famous iconic building." Probably one of the most recognizable buildings in the world, the opera house is made up of two sets of three sail-shaped roofs facing the harbor and smaller ones facing the city. White tiles give it an ability to shimmer in different colors according to the angle of the sunlight and time of day, and also make it a perfect canvas for the annual Festival of Lights, which projects shapes and colors onto the roof. Although mostly likened to white sailboats due to its location by the water, the roof shapes have also been likened to shells and opening lotus leaves.

It was designed by Danish architect Jørn Utzon, whose design was nearly too ambitious for the times, with many redesigns necessary before the unique structure could be realized. Utzon resigned due to quarrels over design, schedules, and costs before he could see the entire project through. He was not in attendance for the grand opening in 1973, but he was rehired in 1999 to develop a set of design principles to act as a guide for all future changes to the building. The building is still a stunning example of the impossible possibilities of architecture, and it is a record-breaking accumulation of statistics: It cost $102 million to build (between 1957 and 1973), over one million tiles shimmer on the roof, some 1,000 rooms play host to 3,000 annual events

The Rocks

HIGH LANE
THE LANGHAM HOTEL
KENT ST
To Napoleon on Kent
SYDNEY OBSERVATORY
WATSON RD
UPPER FORT ST
WINDMILL ST
ARGYLE ST
POTTINGER ST
HICKSON RD
LOWER FORT ST
Walsh Bay
PIER 4
DAWES POINT
SEBEL PIER ONE SYDNEY HARBOUR
PIER 1
SHANGRI-LA HOTEL
SYDNEY HARBOUR YHA
SUSANNAH PLACE MUSEUM
GLOUCESTER ST
CUMBERLAND ST
WESTERN DISTRIBUTOR FWY
CAMBRIDGE ST
ANANAS
THE ROCKS
PYLON LOOKOUT
BRIDGECLIMB
HARRINGTON ST
HARBOUR ROCKS HOTEL
VINTAGE CAFÉ
RENDEZVOUS HOTEL SYDNEY
SUEZ CANAL
SYDNEY VISITOR CENTRE
THE ROCKS DISCOVERY MUSEUM
FINE FOOD STORE
GEORGE ST
THE WOODS/GRAIN
THE RUSSELL HOTEL
NURSES WALK
PHILIP'S FOOTE
BAROQUE
HICKSON RD
First Fleet Park
MUSEUM OF CONTEMPORARY ART
CADMAN'S COTTAGE
BAR 100
PARK HYATT SYDNEY
Dawes Point Park
SYDNEY HARBOUR BRIDGE
Campbells Cove
CAHILL EXPRESSWAY
QUAY/OVERSEAS PASSENGER TERMINAL
CRUISE BAR
6
5
4
3
2
CIRCULAR QUAY
MANLY FERRY
CIRCULAR QUAY
Sydney Cove
SYDNEY COVE OYSTER BAR
PORTOBELLO CAFFE
CIRCULAR QUAY EAST
MACQUARIE ST
MACQUARIE STREET
ARIA
HARBOUR TUNNEL
OPERA BAR
GOVERNMENT HOUSE
Royal Botanic Gardens
SYDNEY OPERA HOUSE
Bennelong Point
0
200 yds
0
200 m
© AVALON TRAVEL

watched by two million people, plus 200,000 tourists visit the opera house each year.

Several guided one-hour tours are offered daily 9am-5pm in various languages, and at noon there's one for visitors with limited mobility.

Writers' Walk

All around Circular Quay, from the opera house past the ferries to The Rocks, are metallic plaques set into the pavement celebrating journalists, poets, writers, and authors from Australia and around the world for their work celebrating Australia, its history, culture, and people. There are greats such as Charles Darwin, quoted as saying "This is really a wonderful colony; ancient Rome in her Imperial grandeur, would not have been ashamed of such an offspring" (letter from Charles Darwin, 1836). Another is Nevil Shute, with the quote "'It's a funny thing,' Jean said. 'You go to a new country, and you expect everything to be different, and then you find there's such a lot that stays the same'" (*A Town Like Alice,* 1950).

Each writer is named, with dates of birth and death where applicable, quotes from their works, and details about their lives and published efforts. Plaques commemorate other writers, such as Peter Carey, Germaine Greer, Robert Hughes, Clive James, Thomas Keneally, D. H. Lawrence, Jack London, Mark Twain, and many more.

The Museum of Contemporary Art

In a prime location on Circular Quay opposite the opera house, **The Museum of Contemporary Art** (140 George St., tel. 02/9245-2400, www.mca.com.au, daily 10am-5pm, Thurs. until 9pm, free) has constantly new and exciting exhibitions highlighting Australian and international art in its rooms. There are daily workshops, performances, talks, and ever-changing events that cover all aspects and dimensions of contemporary art. The large museum offers visitors an extremely wide array of modern art ranging from video installations to palm-front woven fishing traps (they are really quite individual pieces of art in themselves), from paintings to photographs and everything in between. It is a great place to hang out, stop off at the café on the top floor for a rest before taking in another room full of modern delights.

Cadman's Cottage

Built and cut into the natural rock shelf in

The Museum of Contemporary Art

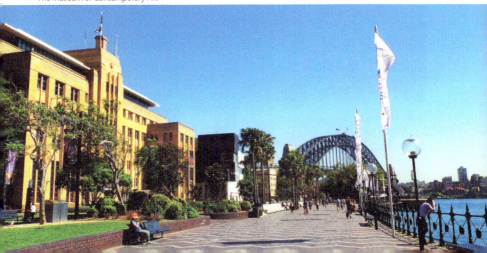

1816, **Cadman's Cottage** (110 George St., tel. 02/9253-0888, Tues.-Sun. 10am-4:30pm, free admission) is one of only a handful of Sydney buildings that remain from the first 30 years of the colony. Over the years this sandstone cottage has been a coxswain's barracks, a sailors' home, and from 1845 the headquarters of the Sydney Water Police, among others. It used to be right beside the water, with its own sandy beach, but since the construction of Circular Quay, the water levels of the harbor have moved 100 meters away.

Suez Canal

The little alleyway between George Street and Harrington Street, opposite the Museum of Contemporary Art, was called the Suez Canal, allegedly after a colloquialism and pun on "sewers." Once a notorious stretch in The Rocks famed for drug abuse, prostitution, and a hangout for gangsters in the 19th century, it is a narrow passageway now decorated with images of "larrikins," a word that reportedly was first recorded in 1868, meaning a "young urban rough, a young hooligan or thug, especially one who is a member of a gang." Alight carefully onto bustling George Street, surprising unsuspecting passersby.

Nurses Walk

Today, Nurses Walk, between Suez Canal and Globe Street, is a bustling lane full of galleries and restaurants; historically it was the shortcut used by nurses to the young colony's first hospital, established together with numerous tent-like out buildings between 1788 and 1816. Formerly located on George Street, in the block bounded by Globe, George, Harrington and Argyle Streets, the hospital is today remembered with a plaque on the nearby former police station at 127 George Street, and the alleyway was renamed Nurses Walk in the 1970s as a tribute to the hospital.

The Rocks Discovery Museum

Housed in a restored 1850s building, **The Rocks Discovery Museum** (2-8 Kendall Ln., tel. 02/9240-8680, daily 10am-5pm, free) is informative, fun, interactive, and full of historical artifacts, pictures, and bits and pieces that bring the history of the surroundings to life. Whether broken rum bottles and glasses from 200 years ago, or shards of a family's crockery, or old toys, leftovers from a bygone era bring that era so much closer to the present. The rooms separate the time periods, which are Warrane (pre-1788), Colony (1788-1820), Port (1820-1900), and Transformations

Cadman's Cottage

(1900-present). The appeal of this little place is that it is certainly informative, but not overwhelmingly so, and it is right in the heart of the place it is telling the story about.

Dawes Point Park

Dawes Point Park is under the Sydney Harbour Bridge on the southern side of the harbor. The Southern Pylon is positioned in the park, and the park has a heritage and historical significance. Originally named Tar-ra by the indigenous people, the park was the site of Sydney's first fortification, built in 1788, although the fortification was removed when construction of Sydney Harbour Bridge began. The Dawes Point Battery was manned until 1916, and today five cannons remain on display in the park. Also a vantage point for the New Year's celebrations, the little park offers fantastic views and now is near the starting point for the BridgeClimb.

Sydney Harbour Bridge

The "coat hanger," as it is affectionately known, has dominated Sydney's harbor skyline since it was opened in 1932. Before then, to cross the relatively narrow gap between Dawes Point and Milsons Point, people needed to travel by one of the many ferries; with boatmen, who navigated smaller, often private, vessels across the harbor; or make an extended trip around the harbor foreshores toward Parramatta and back. To reduce the travel involved, the building of a bridge was proposed as early as 1815, but it was not until 1924 that work first began on the Sydney Harbour Bridge. For the construction of the pylons on both points, some 800 families living in its path, especially around the crowded Rocks, were displaced. Compensation was paid to the owners of the demolished houses, but the occupants, whose homes they were, received nothing.

On January 19, 1932, the first test train, a steam locomotive, safely crossed the bridge. About 90 others also crossed the bridge in the months that followed, as part of a series of tests to ensure the bridge's safety. After the bridge was deemed safe and finished, eventually the construction work sheds, which once occupied the land where you can now find Luna Park and the North Sydney swimming baths, were demolished, and the construction sites were tidied up.

When the Sydney Harbour Bridge was finally opened on March 19, 1932, it was the longest single-span steel-arch bridge in the world. The main span of 503 meters (1,650 feet) across used up more than 52,800 metric tons of silicon-based steel trusses, and the steel plates are held together by around six million steel rivets. From start to finish, the bridge and its approaches took eight years to complete, with a total financial cost of £10,057,170, in old money (roughly 500 times that in modern pounds sterling). This was not fully paid off until 1988.

The initial toll charged for a car was 6 pence while a horse and rider was charged 3 pence. Today the toll, only charged southbound, costs $4 maximum per day. More than 160,000 vehicles cross the bridge each day; before the Harbour Tunnel was opened this figure was as high as 182,000. The Sydney Harbour Bridge carries eight traffic lanes and two railroad lines. There is a pedestrian pathway on the eastern side of the bridge and a cycleway on the western side of the bridge. Pedestrians, horses, and nonmotorized bicycles are not allowed on the bridge roadways.

Located in the southeastern pylon is a **Pylon Lookout** (tel. 02/9240-1100, www.pylonlookout.com.au, daily 10am-5pm, closed Christmas Day, adult $13, child 5-12 $6.50, under 5 free) with 360-degree views and a museum covering the history of the Sydney Harbour Bridge.

★ BRIDGECLIMB

The best way to really appreciate the bridge is to climb it. There are about 200 steps to get to the top, but the views are some of the best in Sydney. **BridgeClimb** (3 Cumberland St., The Rocks, tel. 02/8274-7777, www.bridgeclimb.com.au, from $198 adult, $148 child midweek at night up to $308 adult, $208 child weekend at dawn or twilight) offers four "ways" to climb the bridge. There is really only one route, but the time of day creates four different experiences: You can go at dawn and maybe not quite catch sunrise (but close to it) or at twilight and catch the sunset. You can go in the middle of the day and be one of those strings of ants people point at from the ferries, or you can go up at night and watch magic happen over lit-up Sydney. Each time has its own advantages and disadvantages, so think what suits you and book ahead, as certain times, such as the night climb, have severely restricted numbers.

Once checked in, climbers are thoroughly briefed by the experienced staff about the possible dangers and dos and don'ts during the climb. You'll get suited up in a special "bridge suit" worn over your normal clothes, not only to protect you from the worst of the weather and from getting your clothing snagged, but also to protect the people crossing the bridge underneath you from falling debris. Then you get into a harness and will be wired up with communication equipment. You have to leave cameras and phones behind. Then you go on the climb simulator, to learn a little more about how to behave on the bridge before you are let loose on the real thing. Finally, you are attached to a static line for the duration of the climb, on which you follow a professionally trained climb leader to the top. It takes around three hours to get to the top and back, so you need a good head for heights and a bit of fitness. Be prepared for wind, too—you will be 134 meters (almost 420 feet) above sea level. You will get a photograph of yourself and the group at the top of the bridge.

Note: Climbers must be over 10 years old and more than 102 centimeters (40 inches) in height. If you are up to 24 weeks pregnant, you'll need a doctor's certificate to climb; if you are more than 24 weeks pregnant you can't participate. You will be tested with a Breathalyzer and only allowed up if your blood-alcohol reading is below 0.05. Bring sensible shoes, comfortable clothes, and a sense of adventure.

Susannah Place Museum

Built in 1844 by Irish immigrants, the four terraced houses at **Susannah Place Museum** (58/64 Gloucester St., tel. 02/9241-1893, tours adult $8, child $4, family $17) have been continuously lived in by working-class families and survived largely unchanged through the slum clearances of the early 20th century and the area's dramatic redevelopment in the

BridgeClimb

1970s. They did become increasingly uninhabitable, and in 1990 the museum was set up with the aim to save the buildings and tell the story of the "forgotten" working-class people who helped build Sydney and its wealth. The rooms were left as they used to be, or were restored to their former reality, complete with plates on the table, an old piano playing tunes, toys lying around. You can learn about the tenants of each of the houses, who they were, what they did, how they lived, down to the laundry and the outdoor toilet, and even their favorite brands of food items on sale in the shop.

Admission is by guided tour only, with one-hour tours daily starting at 2pm, 3pm, and 4pm. The tours tell you about the real people who lived in these very houses, and although the buildings are too small to offer actors re-enacting the realities of life then, there are points where you can hear the actual voices of the former tenants telling you about their daily lives in young Sydney.

Sydney Observatory

A beautiful historic building set in a beautiful historic spot, the **Sydney Observatory** (Watson Rd., Observatory Hill, tel. 02/9921-3485, www.sydneyobservatory.com.au, daily 10am-5pm, free daytime admission to gardens and observatory exhibition) offers not only the things you can do inside the observatory, but also the views across the entire harbor, the bridge, and all across Sydney. Built in 1858, the observatory is an astronomical observatory, a timekeeper, a signal station and meteorology center, and a museum with regular and changing exhibitions in keeping with its history. Amazing collections display early astronomical photos, including some of the first photos taken of stars in the southern hemisphere (dating back to 1890) as well as images of a lunar eclipse in 1906. Notice the great golden ball on the pole on the top of the tower. This ball has since 1858 been used as Sydney's timekeeper, being to this day raised at 12:55pm and lowered at 1pm, allowing the people of Sydney and ships' captains to set their chronometers accordingly.

There are daily telescope and planetarium sessions, and a 3-D theater shows both short films and interactive videos about space exploration and astronomy. Day charges for telescope and 3-D theater sessions are adult $10, child $8, family $26. Night telescope sessions are offered April-September at 6:15pm and 8:15pm, October-November at 8:15pm, December-January 8:30pm, and

the Sydney Observatory

February-March at 8:15pm (adult $18, child $12, family $50). An iPhone walking tour app ($1.99) guides you around the site of the observatory down to the Rocks Discovery Museum, past various historical points of interest.

★ Manly Ferry

It is not often that a commuter service is listed as a must-do sight in a guidebook—it is, after all, just a water bus, departing every 30 minutes on a 40-minute one-way trip. Yet the **Manly ferry** (departs from Wharf 3 at Circular Quay, $14.40 round-trip, free with a MyMulti daily or weekly pass) is so much more. Yes, in the morning and afternoon it carries workers between the northern beaches and the city, people who don't necessarily appreciate the views from the ferry, but in between rush hours and on the weekend, this ferry is a perfect way to get out on the water, see the islands, appreciate the view across the opera house and the bridge from the water, take in the mind-blowingly beautiful real estate along the coast, and sit back and enjoy being out on the harbor for a fraction of the price of a harbor cruise. And as a bonus, you get to go to Manly, with its bustling Corso, the partly pedestrianized shopping street connecting the ferry terminal with the beach, full of restaurants and shops, and its beach, which many say is a better surfing beach than the famous Bondi Beach. The jury is still out on that, but the beach is stunning and certainly should be on your list of day trips.

The ferry service runs roughly 6am-midnight. On weekdays, the first ferry leaves Circular Quay at 5:30am, leaves Manly at 6:10am; the last one leaves Circular Quay at 11:45pm, Manly at 12:20am. On weekends, the first ferry leaves Manly at 6:35am, Circular Quay at 6:20am; the last one leaves Manly at 11:40pm, Circular Quay at 11pm.

An alternative **fast ferry** ($9 each way, Wharf 6 at Circular Quay, Manly East Terminal, every 30 minutes) takes only half the time of the regular one but also has half as much character and enjoyment. It is, however, a great option if you need to rush back or the weather has turned.

For more information, check out the **NSW Transport Info** website, www.transportnsw.info, or call tel. 13/15-00.

CENTRAL BUSINESS DISTRICT (CBD)

The city's center, or Central Business District (CBD), with its towering skyscrapers and large colonial buildings, sits on the south side of the harbor and stretches from the busy ferry port of Circular Quay down to the railway hub of Central Station, bordering the chic residential areas of Woolloomooloo and Darlinghurst on the east and Darling Harbour on the west. The CBD is not, as the name might suggest, merely a business district, although most of the head offices of international and national companies can be found here. It is also the central shopping district, full of restaurants, cafés, and most of the museums. It's basically the center of the city, where everything happens during the day, but it gets a little quieter in the evening.

The Australian Museum

The Australian Museum (6 College St., CBD, tel. 02/9320-6000, www.australianmuseum.net.au, daily 9:30am-5pm, adult $12, child 5-15 $6, family $30) is on the corner of College Street and William Street, opposite St. Mary's Cathedral, across the road from Hyde Park. Founded in 1827, the museum is Australia's first and largest natural science museum, housed in an impressive sandstone building complete with Corinthian pillars. Permanent exhibits include a collection of Australian wildlife, including big (dead) spiders; a room on Aboriginal culture and art; a skeleton room; dinosaur displays; and a geology exhibit with replicas of some of the largest gold nuggets found in Australia (would you believe 71.06 kilograms/156 pounds?) and other earthly gems. Regular one-off exhibitions, set up in a separate room with additional entrance fees, have in the past included deep sea exhibits and treasures of Alexander

Free in Sydney

Sydney is expensive—there is no doubt about that. Yet there are a few excellent things to do that don't cost a thing.

- One of the best freebies is the free entry to the **Art Gallery of New South Wales** in the Domain. It is one of the country's, if not the world's, best art galleries, offering art from ancient China right through to modern Australia. The Yiribana Gallery downstairs focuses on Aboriginal and Islander art and offers free guided tours Tuesday-Saturday at 11am.

- The excellent **Museum of Contemporary Art** at The Rocks offers free entry, except for one-off special exhibitions and events that may have a separate charge.

- The free **Rocks Discovery Museum** tells the history of The Rocks from its Aboriginal origins up through today. There are interactive things to do for the kids, combining the teaching of history with the marvels of modern technology.

- **Government House,** the former residence of New South Wales governors in the Royal Botanic Gardens just off Macquarie Street, offers free guided tours every half hour Friday-Sunday 10:30am-3pm, showing you around the interior furnishings and art collections.

- Lovely **St. Mary's Cathedral,** by Hyde Park, offers free cathedral tours every Sunday at noon, and the crypt with its mosaic floor is open daily 10am-4pm.

- Check out the astronomy displays by day at Australia's oldest existing observatory, **Sydney Observatory,** in The Rocks. The Observatory exhibition, access to the building itself, and gardens are free during the daytime and are open daily 10am-5pm. Unfortunately, nighttime tours do have a fee.

- Interested in literature? Follow the **Writers' Walk** along the cobbled streets of The Rocks and along the promenade of Circular Quay, and read the 50 plaques celebrating Australian writers and critics such as Robert Hughes, Germaine Greer, Thea Astley, Peter Carey, Dorothy Hewitt, and James A. Michener.

- You can climb the famous **Sydney Harbour Bridge,** but that costs you. If instead you walk across it, for free (unlike the cars, which have to pay a toll), you get pretty much the same views and superb photo opportunities.

- **Customs House** is a grand historic building with an interesting interior, a library of more than 500,000 books, and a mini-Sydney under a glass dome downstairs. And free Wi-Fi throughout is an added bonus.

- The **Sydney Conservatorium of Music** invites you to listen to its Lunchbreak series during the academic year, with free classical music every Wednesday. See http://music.sydney.edu.au/event-listings for the schedule.

- Take a ride on **bus 555,** which is a free shuttle bus that will take you up and down George Street in the CBD between Railway Square and Circular Quay. It is not only a great way to see the grand buildings lining George Street but also saves time and money if you are shuttling between sights. Check the timetable and route at www.131500.com.au.

the Great. A permanent department offers hands-on science for kids on level two.

Hyde Park

Hyde Park (between Elizabeth, Park, and College Streets) is Australia's oldest park, and although a lot smaller than the original park in London, it is still an oasis within the bustling city, full of interesting sights and surrounded by splendid historical buildings. At the south end there is the **Emden Cannon,** erected to commemorate

Central Business District (CBD)

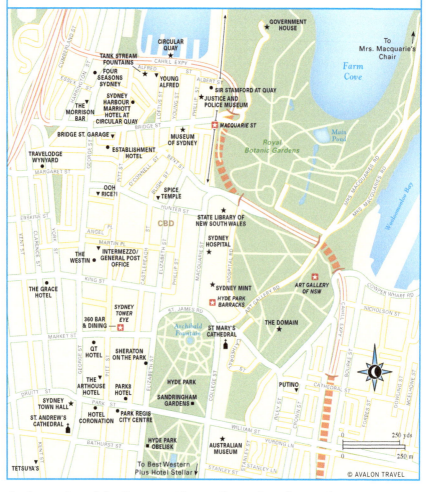

the destruction of the German raider *Emden* on November 9, 1914. The **ANZAC Memorial** is a stunning Art Deco shrine to those lost in the Great War, a peaceful, beautiful shrine that overlooks the Pool of Remembrance.

The **Hyde Park Obelisk,** by Elizabeth Street, was commissioned by the Mayor George Thornton and the Sydney City Council in the mid-1850s as a vent for the noxious gases from the sewer system. Modeled on Cleopatra's Needle in London, it was soon dubbed "Thornton's Scent Bottle."

Across Park Street are the **Sandringham Gardens.** Dedicated to both King George V and King George VI, these tiny sunken gardens, with terraces leading down to a reflecting pool in the center, have pergolas over the circular walk around the garden that, in spring, are cascading with wisteria. An avenue leads up to **Archibald's Fountain,** lined by ancient trees with grazing ibis scuttling through grass underneath. The stone fountain itself is a veritable zoo, with water-squirting bronze turtles, minotaurs being slain, horses, deer, and hounds looking on. It's a feast of 1930s style, conceived and erected by Parisian sculptor François Sicard. It was gifted by Australian journalist and publisher J. F. Archibald to commemorate the association of Australia and France in World War I.

St. Mary's Cathedral

St. Mary's Cathedral (St. Mary's Rd., tel. 02/9220-0400, www.stmaryscathedral.org.au, Sun.-Fri. 6:30am-6:30pm, Sat. 8am-6:30pm) is the seat of the Archbishop of Sydney. The largest cathedral in the city, it is a working church with traditional bell-ringers. A beautiful mass held at Christmas is attended by more than 1,000 worshippers.

The first St. Mary's foundation stone was laid by Governor Macquarie in 1821 and blessed by Father John Therry, one of Australia's first official priests. Work on extensions to the cathedral commenced in 1851 to designs by A. W. N. Pugin, a celebrated English architect and promoter of a more correct Gothic style. Sadly, the cathedral was destroyed by fire in 1865, and Archbishop Polding, the first Archbishop of Sydney, immediately commissioned William Wardell to design a new one. A temporary building was constructed but burned down in 1869.

Work began on the new cathedral in 1866 and took more than 30 years to complete. The incomplete northern section opened in 1882, and the entire church was finished in 1900. It's an outstanding example of Gothic Revival architecture, with the facade based on Paris's Notre Dame Cathedral.

Mary MacKillop, who in the 19th century established an order to educate Australia's rural poor, in 2010 became the first and only Australian to be canonized a saint. A statue of her stands on the city side of the building. St. Mary's does have the greatest length of any church in Australia and is famed for its colorful stained glass windows depicting numerous scenes relating to the life of Jesus, the saints, and, of course, Mary. The screen behind the altar is carved from Oamaru stone from New Zealand.

★ Macquarie Street

Macquarie Street (stretching between Hyde Park and the Sydney Opera House) is named after Lachlan Macquarie, who was governor of New South Wales between 1810 and 1821, and undoubtedly one of the most eminent and celebrated figures in Australian history. He had a vision for Sydney and carried it out: Macquarie Street was designed to be a ceremonial thoroughfare, on the eastern border of Sydney's CBD, and the border of the easy-to-maneuver grid system. Under Macquarie's guidance, many important historical buildings were located along this important street, starting with **St. James Church** (Sydney's oldest church, dating back to 1819, originally built as a courthouse, with an interesting copper dome inside), the **Hyde Park Barracks,** and **Sydney Hospital,** which were built when he was governor. **Parliament House,** the **State Library,** the **Sydney Conservatorium of Music,** and **Government House** followed later but are very much in keeping with the overall grandeur of the street, as is the **Sydney Opera House.**

Parliament House is still a working governmental building, housing the New South Wales Legislative Assembly; it's open to public (Mon.-Fri. 9am-5pm, free tour at 1pm on the first Thurs. of the month except when the assembly is in session).

Opposite the eminent state buildings, which are on the eastern side of Macquarie Street, are other architecturally important and beautiful buildings, such as the Old Colonial Regency-style Hornbury Terrace building (173 Macquarie St.), dating back to 1842, and the stunning Art Deco building housing the British Medical Association (135 Macquarie St.), just opposite the Palace Gates to the Botanic Garden. Many of the buildings are either private or used as offices, but the British Medical Association building has a tiny coffee shop on the ground floor, which allows you to peek into the building under the pretense of getting a sandwich: **Beans at Becs** (135 Macquarie St., tel. 02/9251-1137, weekdays 5:30am-3pm) has great made-to-order sandwiches for $7.

★ Hyde Park Barracks

Formerly an immigration depot, an asylum, and offices for various governmental departments, the **Hyde Park Barracks** (Queens Square, Macquarie St., tel. 02/8239-2311, www.hht.net.au, daily 10am-5pm, adult $10, child $5, family $20) started life as night lodgings for convicts who were laboring on public works in Sydney back in 1817. The Old Colonial Georgian-style building offered an alternative lodging and life for the working convicts away from the higgledy-piggledy living in The Rocks but also provided the government control over the convicts when they were not at work. The museum tells the story of those convicts very intimately—you can inspect the "ratacombs," the tunnels the rats were building under the floors and which were only discovered recently; learn about the convicts' meal rations; hear the story of the formidable Lucy Hicks, the live-in matron of the barracks, a woman who struggled to combine her intense work load with raising her 14 children in the 1870s; and find evidence of the elusive water source known as the Tank Stream. Ticket price includes a free audio guide. Allow around two hours for a self-guided tour covering most points.

Sydney Mint

Next to Hyde Park Barracks, the **Sydney Mint** (10 Macquarie St., tel. 02/8239-2288, www.hht.net.au, Mon.-Fri. 9am-5pm, free admission) was originally established to control the black market and prevent financial disaster after the discovery of gold in New South Wales. Operating between May 1855 and December 1926, the mint produced gold sovereigns and other coinage, over its 70 years processing more than 1,200 tons of gold and producing more than 150 million sovereigns. The elegant colonnaded colonial-style building, with a contemporary building behind it, is beautifully lighted at night and today serves as a library and houses a simple historical display. Notably, the Caroline Simpson Library holds the only public research collection dedicated to the history of the home and garden in Australia. Lovely little **Bullion Bar** (Wed.-Fri. 3pm-9pm) is perfect for a relaxing drink between cultural explorations.

Sydney Hospital

The oldest hospital in Australia, **Sydney Hospital** (8 Macquarie St., tel. 02/9382-7111) originally dates back to the arrival of the First Fleet in 1788, when it was dubbed "Rum Hospital." When the British government refused to provide money to build a hospital, Governor Macquarie entered into a business arrangement with three individuals who saw the opportunity to turn the governor's need for a hospital to their financial advantage. They reportedly undertook the building of the hospital if given a monopoly to import rum into the colony.

The hospital has been in the current location since 1811. A working hospital, it is not generally open to the public, but small parts, such as **The Little Shop** (Mon.-Fri. 10:30am-2:30pm), selling hand-made children's clothes and toys to the public, allow a small glimpse behind the facade. The Little Shop is staffed by volunteers and set up by the main entrance in the old gate house. There is also the lucky boar fountain, **Il Porcellino,** presented to the city in 1968 by Marchesa Torrigiani of Florence in memory of her father, Brigadier General Thomas Fiaschi. It's a replica of the original 1547 statue found in the Straw Market in Florence. Legend has it that it is lucky to rub the boar's nose and donate a coin toward the hospital. You'll find it just outside the main entrance on Macquarie Street.

The best view of the many architectural styles can be appreciated from the hospital's courtyard. The Nightingale Wing, home to the oldest nursing school in the country, is, after many reconstructions, the oldest part of the building now, dating back to 1868 and held in Gothic Revival style. It is joined by the main building, dating back to 1894, and other smaller wings, all of which are in distinctly different styles and surround the magnificent three-tiered cast-iron Robert Brough Memorial Fountain from the Colebrookdale, United Kingdom, factory, installed in 1907. **Courtyard Café da Capo** (tel. 02/9382-7359, Mon.-Fri. 7:30am-4pm), a quiet little Italian coffee shop in the courtyard, seemingly a million miles away from the bustle of Macquarie Street, allows you to savor the beauty of Sydney Hospital over a quiet drink.

State Library of New South Wales

The **State Library of New South Wales** (Bent St., corner Macquarie St., tel. 02/9273-1414, Mon.-Thurs. 9am-8pm, Fri. 9am-5pm, Sat. 10am-5pm, free) traces its origins to 1826, with the opening of the Australian Subscription Library. In 1869, the New South Wales government took over responsibility for the library and created the Sydney Free Public Library. In 1895 it was renamed the Public Library of New South Wales, and in 1975 it became the State Library of New South Wales.

The old part of the state library on Bent Street, looking like an ancient Greek temple, houses the Mitchell Library, opened in 1910. The foyer displays the marble copy of the original Tasman Map, which combines the results of Tasman's first (1642 to 1643) and second (1644) voyages with those of earlier Dutch navigators, showing a surprisingly accurate general outline of Australia. Princess George of Greece presented the original Tasman Map to the library in 1931, where it is kept under lock and key.

A quote from Thomas Carlyle in the entrance hall, "In Books lies the soul of the whole past time/The articulate audible voice of the past when the body and material substance of it has altogether vanished like a dream," gives a clue as to the importance of the library, and for book-lovers the Mitchell Reading Room in its understated elegance, lined with several stories of bookshelves concluding in a glass ceiling, is simply stunning.

The Domain

The Domain (Mrs Macquaries Rd., CBD) surrounds the Royal Botanic Gardens and was in colonial times the governor's buffer of privacy between his residence and the penal colony. Roads and paths were constructed throughout the Domain in 1831 to allow public access, somewhat ruining the governor's privacy, and the Domain has since been a place for the people. There is even a sign advising keen hobby gardeners on how to keep their own lawn green and healthy in times of drought. In the spirit of public enjoyment, this 34-hectare open garden space is a popular venue for concerts, festivals, open-air events, and, at Christmastime, the very popular **Carols in the Domain.** The manicured lawns invite you to picnic, take in the views, or use the expanse of walkways for exercise.

★ Art Gallery of New South Wales

Looking like a Greek temple from the front, sitting dominant on the Domain with lovely views across Woolloomooloo Bay, the **Art Gallery of New South Wales** (Art Gallery Rd., The Domain, tel. 1800/679-278, www.artgallery.nsw.gov.au, daily 10am-5pm, free) is a fantastic collection of art, stretching from old European collections to modern Australian works, ancient Asian art, and Aboriginal and Torres Strait Islander art. There are three permanent exhibitions: Australian, 15th to 19th century European, and Asian. Very aptly, the older works, such as those by Constable, Rubens, and Canaletto, are housed in the original building dating back to 1871, and the newer works are housed in the modern wing at the back. The old wing is a stunning space complete with vaulted ceilings, parquet flooring, and many historical features that do not take away from but instead enhance the art on display. The modern rooms are used perfectly to showcase installations, paintings, sculptures, and much more.

On the lower level, there is an incredible collection of ancient Asian art, showcasing a panorama of 7,000-odd years of Chinese and Asian art evolution, including ceramics dating to the period 206 BCE to 220 CE. Beautiful porcelains, examples of Japanese calligraphy, and day-to-day objects make for a stunning collection.

Regular traveling exhibitions (which may incur an entrance fee), talks and lectures by visiting artists, and workshops make this into one of the best museum/galleries in the country.

The Royal Botanic Gardens

Not unlike Central Park in New York, **The Royal Botanic Gardens** (eastern edge of the CBD, bordered by Macquarie St., the Cahill Expressway, and Mrs Macquarie Rd., tel. 02/9231-8111, Nov.-Feb. daily 7am-8pm, Mar. and Oct. daily 7am-6:30pm, Apr. and Sept. daily 7am-6pm, May and Aug. daily 7am-5:30pm, June-July daily 7am-5pm, free) are the lungs of Sydney, a place to rest, relax, exercise, bring the family, grab some culture, and enjoy the surroundings. Signs actually encourage visitors to "walk on the grass," which is always a positive thing.

What started as a few paths cut through the native shrubby vegetation back in 1816 is now a 30-hectare parkland full of native and foreign plants and also is the oldest scientific institution in Australia, with research having continuously been carried out over the centuries. Not to be confused with the Domain (the parkland that surrounds the gardens), the Royal Botanic Gardens are a mix of manicured lawns, ancient trees, modern sculptures, and historic monuments placed to enhance the green surroundings and conveniently positioned to allow relaxation and views to come together. You can explore the rare and threatened plants from around the globe and learn about the Cadigal (the original inhabitants of Sydney's city center) and their relationship with this land at Cadi Jam Ora—First Encounters, a special garden display. Rose gardens and unique plants set among some of the best views in the world make this a great place to relax.

One of the best spots of all of Sydney is **Mrs Macquarie's Chair,** right at the tip of the Royal Botanic Gardens jutting out into the harbor, reportedly the place the governor's wife chose to retreat to to watch the world go by. A benchlike shape hewn out of the sandstone rock in 1810 by convicts, it's a great viewing point.

The gardens stretch around pretty Farm Cove, with the famous Fleet Steps, which have been taken even by Queen Elizabeth II, leading down to the water's edge. Within the botanic gardens are the historic Government House and the Sydney Conservatorium of Music, both situated along the border with Macquarie Street.

Government House

Architect Edward Blore of Buckingham Palace fame was heavily involved in the design of this impressive Gothic Revival castellated **Government House** (Royal Botanic Gardens/Macquarie St., tel. 02/9931-5222, grounds open daily 10am-4pm, house tours Fri.-Sun. 10:30am-3pm, free), which is still

---

Admission Fees

You will find mention of **"family admission"** in most sights and attractions around Australia. This generally refers to a group made up of two adults and two children. Just to confuse the issue, some attractions, such as Tarongo Zoo, also offer a family ticket for two adults and three children, but generally speaking a family group is two adults and two children, and this group ticket always works out cheaper than separate tickets.

You will also see **"concession" tickets** on most signs. This refers to students, senior citizens, and those with disabilities. To be entitled to these reduced admission fees you will need to provide valid proof—a current card or pass, generally with a photograph on it—that you are, for example, a student.

part of the small Tank Stream exhibit in the basement of the General Post Office Building

a working state house and has been home to governors since it was opened in 1846, when it took over from the first Government House, remains of which can be seen at the Museum of Sydney. Inside, each governor has made changes according to their tastes, and the state rooms display a vast array of 19th- and 20th-century designs. Tours start every 30 minutes and last for around 45 minutes. They are the only way to look inside and learn about the history of the house and the governors, as well as the architecture and design of the house. You can wander around the gardens, taking in the house from the outside, and its general setting, but you'll get more insight through the tours.

Museum of Sydney

The **Museum of Sydney** (corner Bridge St. and Phillip St., tel. 02/9251-5988, www.hht.net.au, daily 10am-5pm, adult $10, child 5, family $20) stands on the site of the first Government House, which was the first major building to be constructed on the Australian mainland, started mere months after the landing of the First Fleet in 1788. The museum tells the story of that building with various paintings and tales. The exhibition moves on to the First Fleet, with details and replicas of each ship in the fleet, continuing with the city's trade history with examples of what was carried on the ships. One fantastic way of displaying various articles is in the great metal chest of drawers, each drawer being a miniature exhibition in its own right: full of broken china, letters, pieces of the life led by the early settlers, tempting you to spend hours looking at details lovingly displayed and allowing a certain intimacy with history. There are also changing exhibitions such as "Food," the story of Sydney told in numerous table settings complete with decor and food as it would have once been set up.

Justice & Police Museum

Located in three historic sandstone police courthouses dating back to 1856, the **Justice & Police Museum** (corner Albert St. and Phillip St., Circular Quay, tel. 02/9252-1144, www.hht.net.au, weekends 10am-5pm, adult $10, child under 15 years $5, family $20) tells the story of Sydney's rogues, vagabonds, and other perps, and the stoic police officers who brought them to justice and kept order in the growing city. Displays of weaponry, items that once belonged to infamous Australian outlaws (or bushrangers, as they are called locally, such as the Ned Kelly Gang), eerie photographs of criminals, and cells allow you to imagine what it was like in a late 1800s prison. You can even inspect real-life forensic evidence that related to two murders in the state.

Tank Stream

The **Tank Stream** (various locations) was one of the main reasons why the landing party from HMS *Supply*, ordered to explore the land by Governor Phillip on January 26, 1788, was deemed so successful. This small stream rising from the murky swamps that are now very civilized Hyde Park offered the vital source of fresh water needed to sustain the first colony.

Named after the four deep storage tanks that were dug into the sandstone base of the stream to ensure the fresh water collected could be used as and when needed, the stream was a precious commodity, appreciated and looked after by means such as 50-foot-wide greenbelts on either side of the stream.

By 1826 the Tank Stream was no longer the main water source, with a new vast reservoir being built in Centennial Park. The stream eventually got covered up, and ended up as a sewage and storm drainage system. But there are still many signs of the historic stream. Start the trail at Circular Quay, where several fountains celebrate the stream, then look for markers on the lanes and in buildings as to the former course. The markers are part of the Tank Stream installation created by artist Lynne Roberts-Goodwin in 1999 and can be found at various points throughout the CBD. Walk to Tank Stream Way, off Bridge Street, named after the bridge across the stream, and peek into 17 Bridge Street, an entrance to an office building where you can see two markers on the floor before the elevators. Go to the old General Post Office Building, now housing the Westin Hotel. In the basement among the bars and cafés, you will find a small, hidden away but publicly accessible exhibition showcasing sections of the brick structure that formerly enclosed the stream and numerous artifacts found in the stream. It is a secret history display that not many people find in the city, yet it pays homage to such an important part of Sydney's history.

Sydney Tower Eye dominating the city's skyline

★ Sydney Tower Eye

The **Sydney Tower Eye** (Level 5, Westfield Mall, Pitt St., tel. 02/9333-9222, www.sydneytowereye.com.au, daily 9am-10:30pm, from adult $18.20, child $10.50, family $54, combo deals available online) should be your first stop on your trip to Sydney. The 309-meter tower took six years and $36 million to build, was completed in 1981, and is still the tallest building in Sydney. Your journey begins with a surprisingly good 4-D cinema experience before you head up, giving you a 10-minute aerial tour of Sydney and surroundings, and the 360-degree viewing platform at the top allows you to get your bearings and appreciate the true beauty and sprawl of the harbor and city. Looking out all the way to the Blue Mountains on the horizon, Botany Bay, and the tiny entrance from the Pacific Ocean that the First Fleet thought worth investigating gives you an appreciation of the natural and man-made beauty of the surroundings. Seeing the parks and the magnificent buildings leaves you raring to go and explore.

If looking down through the glass is simply too boring for you, you can sign up for the Skywalk on the rooftop. Get dressed in blue coveralls, don a safety harness, and walk around the rim of the tower's roof for an hour, stopping off at two glass platforms looking out and down on the ant-like life below (adult $43, child $30, minimum age 8 years old, hourly from 10am). If serenity is more your thing, there are weekly yoga classes up in the tower every Wednesday morning at 7am ($25).

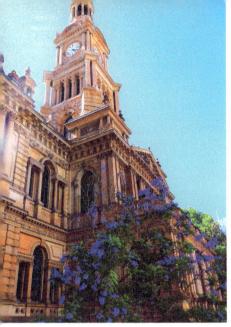

Sydney Town Hall

Sydney Town Hall

Constructed on the site of Sydney's first cemetery, which operated from 1792 to 1820 and was subsequently relocated, the grand **Sydney Town Hall** (483 George St., tel. 02/9265-9333, www.cityofsydneyvenues.com.au, Mon.-Fri. 8:30am-6pm) was built from honey-colored sandstone quarried from nearby Pyrmont. Built after the French Second Empire style, with some influences from Roman and Greek history, the town hall was conceived by architect J. H. Wilson, who, together with subsequent architects working on the project, died during construction, which stretched across the years 1868 to 1889, with the clocktower completed in 1873. Nevertheless, each seemed to have left quirky embellishments throughout the building, maybe trying to leave some of their ideas behind for history. Look for numerous lions on the facade, different styles of windows (some with stained-glass, others clear), and the bridges formed by the raised entrances, at the front and the side.

Inside, the town hall has a majestic vestibule and staircase, and an old-fashioned cage elevator. Inside the Centennial Hall, the Grand Organ was the largest and most magnificent in the world when it was installed in 1890, and regular performances showcase its prowess to the audience.

St. Andrew's Cathedral

Dating back to 1868, **St. Andrew's Cathedral** (corner George St. and Bathurst St., tel. 02/9265-1661, www.sydneycathedral.com, Mon.-Tues. 10am-4pm, Wed. 10am-7:30pm, Thurs. 10am-4pm, Sun. 8am-9pm) is Australia's oldest cathedral, complete with spiky spires and intricate stained-glass windows inspired by York Minster in England. The cathedral itself is not just beautiful but full of interesting bits of history: Near the entrance a copy of the Great Bible can be seen under glass, the original dating back to 1539, when Henry VIII decreed that a copy of the bible printed in English should be displayed in every parish church. Original foundations of the church were uncovered during restoration works to the cathedral in 1999, and a number of foundation plaques commemorate the laying of the foundation stone in 1819 by Governor Lachlan Macquarie. The organ, originally dating back to 1866, and since then updated and altered throughout the years, is still on display with its unusual wrought iron surrounds, and the church holds monthly organ recitals.

DARLING HARBOUR AND HAYMARKET

To the west of Sydney's CBD, Darling Harbour is a pedestrianized entertainment precinct located around Cockle Bay, a busy hub for ferries and pleasure boats. The area is ideal for families, with parks, museums, small trains taking you around the bay, and restaurants lining Cockle Bay Wharf. There is more than enough to keep you busy for an entire day.

Haymarket, just south of Darling Harbour, is home to Sydney's Chinatown, a bustling area full of restaurants, markets, and traditional shops. The neighborhood also features surprisingly quiet and serene parks and playgrounds (one even has an old-fashioned carousel), considering the nearby buzz.

Sea Life Sydney Aquarium

Highlights at **Sea Life Sydney Aquarium** (Aquarium Wharf/1-5 Wheat Rd., Darling Harbour, tel. 02/9333-9288, www.sydneyaquarium.com.au, daily 9am-8pm, last admission at 7pm, adult from $26, child $16, family $65, if booked online; combo deals available online) include turtles, sharks, sea horses, sea dragons, jellyfish, and even a dugong, a sister species of the manatees, among many other fresh- and seawater dwelling creatures from Australia and abroad. The displays are interactive, with plenty of Q&A stations for kids. An excellent display focuses on the Great Barrier Reef, which gives you lots of insight and knowledge about the reef and its critters. There are extra activities you can add onto your visit, such as a glass-bottom boat ride ($10), feeding the sharks ($15), and a behind the scenes look at 11:30am and 2pm daily ($25). Depending on your interests, you can spend easily spend two or three hours here.

Wild Life Sydney Zoo

Next door to Sea Life Sydney is **Wild Life Sydney Zoo** (Aquarium Wharf/1-5 Wheat Rd., Darling Harbour, tel. 02/9333-9288, www.wildlifesydney.com.au, daily 9am-6pm, adult from $26, child $16.80, family $79, if booked online; combo deals available online), where you are greeted by a koala munching on leaves right at the entrance. Go in and meet more of those near-mythical Australian animals: hopping kangaroos, wombats, even a cassowary. And you can get up close to a koala; although here in NSW you are not allowed to hug one, you can get very close and give him a little stroke. (The hugging you will have to leave until Queensland, where it is still legal.) There are snakes, lizards, spiders and nearly two of every creature that hops, crawls and wanders around this vast continent. A fun way to spend a couple of hours for all the family.

> ## Double Up and Save
>
> **Sea Life Sydney Aquarium, Wild Life Sydney Zoo, Madame Tussauds,** and **Sydney Tower Eye** are managed by the same company and offer reduced tickets if you want to visit two or more attractions. See any two of the attractions for adult $65, child $37, family $180; see three attractions for adult $70, child $40, family $195; or see all four for adult $80, child $50, family $240. The deal is well worth considering, especially if you have kids in tow.

Madame Tussauds

There are many museums telling the story of Australia, its history, and its people, and **Madame Tussauds** (Aquarium Wharf/1-5 Wheat Rd., Darling Harbour, tel. 02/9333-9240, www.madametussauds.com/sydney, daily 9am-8pm, last admission at 7pm, adult $40, child $28, family $136, save 30% online; combo deals available online) is doing the same, only it adds fun, modern history, current people you should know, and some gossip. Meet Australia's historic heroes, including Captain Cook and Trugernanner, the last Aboriginal woman to live and die in Tasmania; modern Australian heroes such as aviator Kingsford Smith; world leaders; and achievers and innovators from the fields of science, medicine, music, and film. And while you are learning about Australia, you can join in the fun and look behind the scenes and even have a hand cast done (one hand $20, two hands $25, four hands $40). Allow an hour to go through it all.

Australian National Maritime Museum

Australia's history is nothing if not linked closely with naval and maritime pursuits. Exhibits at the **Australian National Maritime Museum** (2 Martin St., Darling Harbour, tel. 02/9298-3777, www.anmm.gov.au, daily 9:30am-5pm, adult $7, child $3.50,

Darling Harbour and Haymarket

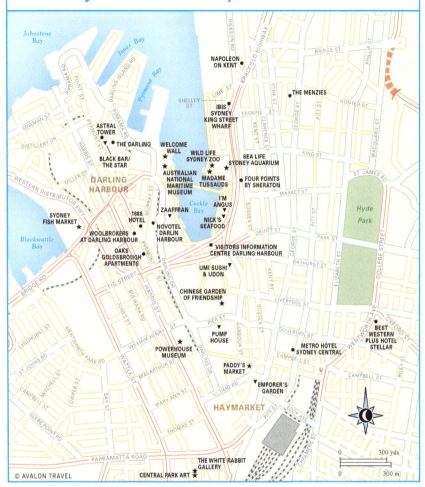

family $17.50, free first Thurs. of the month, extra fee for special exhibitions) go back to Aboriginal history, the First Fleet, explorations of the coast, and more recent wartime history, such as Gallipoli. The museum also has a historic fleet docked outside, and you can venture onboard a naval destroyer and marvel at other visiting vessels, such as a submarine that was in port during writing. Special exhibitions explore history such as that of the Vikings.

Welcome Wall

North of the Australian National Maritime Museum, between Darling Harbour and Pyrmont Bay is the Welcome Wall. Literally a wall, it is inscribed with the names of people who have migrated to Australia. To date there are more than 23,000 names listed, with countries of origin, which add up to over 150 different nations. Obviously this is a mere drop in the bucket where Australia's immigrants are concerned, but it makes interesting reading, whether you personally are looking for a name or not. If you have someone you'd like to be commemorated, you can apply to have your relative added to the list; inquire in the Australian National Maritime Museum for further details.

Darling Harbourside Fireworks

All across Darling Harbour, there are superb fireworks nearly every Saturday night at 9pm. You can watch them from anywhere around the harbor, but if you want to combine dining with the celebrations, you'd better book ahead as the restaurants tend to get busy around that time.

Sydney Fish Market

The **Sydney Fish Market** (Pyrmont Bridge Rd., Pyrmont, tel. 02/9004-1100, www.sydneyfishmarket.com.au, daily 7am until around 4pm, although some outlets and restaurants stay open until late) is a working fish market, so it is by definition smelly, wet, and at times slippery. But if you are interested in fish, be it on your plate or just to check out the variety landed off the Australian coast, a visit to the market is well worth it. With plenty of food stalls and restaurants around the market, you can sample the freshest catches of the day, and if you are inspired to become a seafood chef yourself but don't know where to start, there is even the option to take some cooking classes; just check the calendar for Sydney Seafood School and book ahead at www.sydneyfishmarket.com.au.

Chinese Garden of Friendship

Within bustling Sydney, just by all the busy restaurants south of Darling Harbour lies a haven of serenity, the **Chinese Garden of Friendship** (south of Darling Harbour, opposite the Sydney Entertainment Centre, tel. 02/9240-8888, daily 9:30am-5pm, adult $6, child $3, family $15), a step into another land and culture. The gardens bring together little pagodas, water features, bridges across gurgling streams, sculptures, and carvings. A lovely tea house has excellent scones, or if you'd like to stay with the theme order some dim sim (a dumpling-type dish).

Paddy's Market

Paddy's Market (Thomas St. and Hay St., Haymarket, tel. 02/9325-6200, Wed.-Mon. 9am-5pm) is a gigantic market space offering everything from fresh produce to cheap souvenirs, risqué underwear, makeup, accessories, clothes, toys, absolutely anything else

the Australian National Maritime Museum's mooring in Darling Harbour

you could possibly want, and then some. If you have dozens of friends to take souvenirs back to, then shop here for best deals.

Powerhouse Museum

The **Powerhouse Museum** (500 Harris St., Ultimo, tel. 02/9217-0111, www.powerhousemuseum.com, daily 10am-5pm, adult $12, child $6, family $30) really is a powerhouse of a museum that defies definition. In a vast space you will find entire trains, planes, cars, even space ships. But it is not a transport museum, even though it does have a transport display in one of its many rooms. There are science experiments but it is not a science museum. There are plenty of activities for children, but it is not a children's museum.

There are exhibits such as the "Steam Revolution," set in the original engine room of the Ultimo Powerhouse, where Sydney's first electric trams were generated. A beautiful bright red and brass NSW Fire Brigade water pump used to be pulled by horses and reportedly fought more than 1,000 fires in its time. Then there is the "Experimentations" exhibition, where your kids—and you—can get your hands busy experimenting with anything from smells and tastes to making your own fireworks. Move on and learn about costumes, the history of fashion and clothes-making, shopping habits in early Australian history, and even robots. You can try your hand at maneuvering a virtual Mars rover and try to collect some rock samples. Depending on how hands-on you will get in the museum, allow at least a couple of hours to marvel at all the exhibits.

The White Rabbit Gallery

The White Rabbit Gallery (30 Balfour St., Chippendale, tel. 02/8399-2867, www.whiterabbitcollection.org, Thurs.-Sat. 10am-6pm, free) is not strictly speaking in Haymarket, more on the edge of the district, but given that the gallery houses one of the largest and most important collections of modern Chinese contemporary art, it needs to be included near Chinatown attractions. The gallery not only has a great café and gift shop, but most importantly offers a glimpse into Chinese art and the psyche of some of the artists. Oppression and new-found freedom both rank high in the subject matter, with videos, paintings, and etchings being the typical media; there are also talking plants, traditional imperial clothes recreated from pages cut from a Chinese-English dictionary, and the moving rubble of a destroyed house. Certainly quirky,

modes of transport in the Powerhouse Museum

and a must for anybody interested in contemporary art.

Central Park Art

Just around the corner from the White Rabbit Gallery, **Central Park Art** (off Broadway, Chippendale, south of Central Station) is an amazing $8 million public art collection that has taken over this serene stretch of parkland. Integrated into the architecture surrounding the park, both modern and historical, the art is huge, such as the enormous jutting glass roof sheltering the park below, the animated Hula-Hoop, and the abstract red organic structure growing on the side of the old factory facade. It is impressive and there for everybody to enjoy and marvel at.

KINGS CROSS

Kings Cross is at best bohemian, colorful, and unconventional, and at worst, sleazy and suspect. The former red-light district is still a flamboyant place where pretty much everything goes, but it is also lively, bright, ethnically diverse, and exciting. Here it doesn't matter what your color, religion, gender, or sexual persuasion is—everybody mingles and comes to Kings Cross to have fun. The adjoining areas of **Potts Point, Woolloomooloo** (which surely must be the most intriguingly named suburb of Sydney, together with being the oldest), and **Darlinghurst** have been truly gentrified since the 1990s and now offer some of Sydney's most desirable real estate.

Reportedly, the name Woolloomooloo could have been derived from either *wallamullah,* meaning "place of plenty," or from *wallabahmullah,* referring to a young black kangaroo. In these suburbs, interesting history mingles with sedate suburbia; top restaurants live next to tattoo parlors; the clientele runs the gamut from genteel family to drug addicts and plenty of mostly backpacking overseas visitors. Seedy? Yes, in places. Fun? For sure, throughout. To experience the true diversity of Sydney, there is no better area. Once you see the large Coca-Cola sign, you know you are in the heart of Kings Cross and the vibrant Sydney mix.

Elizabeth Bay House

A lovely example of a former residence with incredible views across the harbor, **Elizabeth Bay House** (7 Onslow Ave., Elizabeth Bay, tel. 02/9356-3022, Fri.-Sun. 11am-4pm, adult $8, child $4, family $17) is hidden in a residential area, down steep lanes and hidden steps, and once you find it, you will probably also find it closed, as it is run by volunteers and on occasion the system fails, but like any good treasure hunt, it's actually the search that is fun. The area is full of incredible private residences.

The white Regency-style house with its colonnaded entrance and elegant features itself is lovely but tells a sad story: From 1826 Colonial Secretary Alexander Macleay had the dream to develop the current site overlooking the gorgeous Elizabeth Bay as a fine landscape garden and to build Elizabeth Bay House. It was widely dubbed "the finest house in colony," but he did not have the funds to see his project through. Macleay's life-long obsession with entomology plus the loss of his government post in 1837 required him to seek numerous loans from his eldest son William, and although this house looks grand, it is unfinished. A mere six years into his stay William foreclosed on his father, effectively forcing him to leave.

Today, when you enter, you can imagine the splendor of having lived here, with the grand spiral staircase winding its way up to the magnificent dome; the finely set dining table ready to host a dinner party; the magnificent library, reportedly once the largest room in any Australian house; and the grand views outside across the bay. The house is sometimes hired out for weddings because of its stylish interior, and you can just imagine a bride coming down the staircase with her dress's train sweeping down behind. For tours, please contact Elizabeth Bay House to arrange one convenient to you, as there are no set times. A tour takes around 45 minutes.

Kings Cross and Paddington

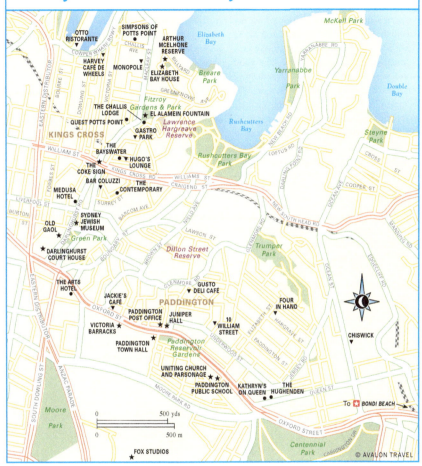

Arthur McElhone Reserve

On Elizabeth Bay House's doorstep lies the tiny hidden **Arthur McElhone Reserve** (Billyard Ave., Elizabeth Bay), a manicured little park with koi ponds and lily pads and stunning views across the harbor. Benches are provided to enjoy the views, and on a warm day, this is definitely the place to bring a sandwich and a book and enjoy the tranquil surroundings.

Breare Park

Breare Park (Ithaca Rd., Elizabeth Bay Marina) is a small but perfectly located park and one of the hot spots for New Year's Eve celebrations because of its stunning views across the harbor. Sailboats are twinkling away in the marina, a small island sits in the bay, and behind are some incredible real state gems. This is a perfect place to take a rest from sightseeing.

Macleay Street and Around

Coming back up from the bay, the varied architecture on display around Potts Point is worth a little look. Walk along Macleay Street, through Challis Avenue, and along Victoria Street before winding your way back to Macleay Street and you will get a good overview of the varied styles of architecture found house to house in Sydney. The gorgeous Victorian lace terrace houses along Victoria Street are set off by the imposing walls of St. Vincent's College for Girls, established back in 1858, whereas in the side streets you'll find interwar architecture and large Georgian villas.

The **El Alamein Fountain** (Fitzroy Gardens, Macleay St.) is an iconic fountain standing as a memorial to the soldiers who died in World War II in Egypt. Designed by Australian architect Bob Woodward, the fountain resembles a large dandelion flower and is set in a small park, which also hosts the **Kings Cross Organic Market** every Saturday (8am-2pm), where Kings Cross showcases fresh organic produce, home-baked sourdough bread, fresh flowers, exotic food stands, and entertainment.

Sydney Jewish Museum

The **Sydney Jewish Museum** (148 Darlinghurst Rd., Darlinghurst, tel. 02/9360-7999, Sun.-Thurs. 10am-4pm, Fri. 10am-2pm, adult $10, child $7, family $22) focuses especially on the experiences of Australian Jews during the Holocaust but also has regular non-Holocaust exhibitions, such as "Jewish Fashion and Art." Guided tours for individual visitors take place at noon Monday, Wednesday, Friday, and Sunday and are about 45 minutes in duration. The museum addresses the history and culture of the Jewish community in Sydney and Australia but also explains the culture, religion, and world history of Judaism.

Old Gaol

The **Old Gaol** (corner Burton St. and Forbes St., Darlinghurst, tel. 02/9339-8744, Mon.-Fri. 9am-5pm) now houses the National Art School, and its thick imposing walls hide a variety of historic buildings inside. The jail was used as a prison between 1840 and 1912. It was originally built for 732 prisoners, including 156 women, but reportedly at one stage 450 women were held there. A total of 79 people were executed there; the last hanging was in October 1908. Even though it's now a college, it is possible to walk around the grounds. There's also a coffee shop run by students and an art supply shop.

the El Alamein Fountain on Macleay Street

Darlinghurst Court House

Together with the Old Gaol next door, the **Darlinghurst Court House** (Forbes St., Darlinghurst, tel. 02/9368-2947, Feb.-Dec. Mon.-Fri. 10am-4pm) and its associated buildings make up an entire block representing the former justice system. The Greek Revival-style building was designed by architect Mortimer Lewis in 1844 and was the first purpose-built courthouse in New South Wales, becoming the template for courthouse design throughout the colony for the next 60 years. Still in use today, the main building was aligned to face directly onto Oxford Street, but the buildings stretch up to Taylor Square, where you can also find the Old Police Station. Check out the public toilet building for some historic background on the square and its buildings, as the bathroom building doubles as an information wall for the local area and its history.

PADDINGTON

Paddington, or "Paddo" as it is colloquially called, is a trendy suburb between Sydney's CBD and Bondi Beach. Developed in the 1820s, it was described by historian Max Kelly as "Sydney's first commuter suburb," because Paddington Village did not have any independent economic life to support its residents. Paddington is now known for its Australian designer fashion shops, the fashion walk (where local fashion icons are immortalized on numerous plaques on the sidewalk), its gorgeous residential homes, comfortable little cafés and bars, antiques shops, markets, and generally great atmosphere. It is an atmospheric place to come, away from the at-times overwhelming amount of history in The Rocks and the CBD, and just "be."

Saunter along the shops, buy some knick-knacks, have a coffee, and grab a sneak peek of how Sydneysiders live in this part of the city. But there is also plenty of history, particularly around the main thoroughfare of Oxford Street, once a "walking track" used by the Aboriginal people, which runs along a ridgeline above most of Paddington. The land within Paddington was once the home of the Cadigal people, who spoke a Dharug dialect of the Aboriginal language, and many of their rituals and stories feature this distinct landscape of a ridge drawing alongside the natural harbor on one side and Botany Bay toward the other with what must have been sensational views to both sides.

Paddington's many historic buildings lining Oxford Street are really best viewed as part of a leisurely stroll down the bustling street, mixing pleasures of history with more modern shopping and culinary delights.

Victoria Barracks

The **Victoria Barracks** (Oxford St., between Greens Rd. and Oatley Rd., tel. 02/8335-5330, museum Thurs. 10am-12:30pm and Sun. 10am-3pm, free tour Thurs. by appointment, $2) were built out of local Hawkesbury sandstone between 1841 and 1849 in the Regency style, and were designed by Lieutenant-Colonel George Barney, who also built Fort Denison and reconstructed Circular Quay. Once located quite far from the city center, the barracks were initially occupied by British troops up until 1870 and then taken over by the New South Wales colonial forces. After the Australian Federation was established in 1901, Victoria Barracks housed the various headquarters responsible for administering and coordinating the military. Between 1931 and 1936 the barracks were home to the Royal Military College of Australia, and from July 1938 to July 1940 they also housed the Command and Staff School.

Today, the Victoria Barracks are home to the Headquarters of Forces Command. Inside, Australia's rich culture is prominently displayed, and parts of the building are open to visitors. You can view weapon displays, medals, and army uniforms from early colonial times through to World War II. And apparently, there is also a resident ghost, called Charlie the Redcoat.

Paddington Post Office

Still a working corner post office, **Paddington Post Office** (246 Oxford St., tel. 13/13-18, Mon.-Fri. 9am-5pm) dates back to 1885 and is associated with the NSW Colonial Architect's Office, which designed and maintained post offices across New South Wales between 1865 and 1890. The pretty Victorian Italianate building has numerous original architectural features, such as the colonnaded entrance, high ceilings, and the colorful emblem under the roof. It's as popular today as it was when first built.

Paddington Town Hall

The Victorian Italianate **Paddington Town Hall** (249 Oxford St., tel. 02/9265-9198), just opposite the post office, was completed in 1890. It towers over the Paddington skyline, the large clock tower reportedly symbolizing peace among nations. Today the town hall hosts a library, radio stations, and a cinema, and is often a venue for private functions.

Juniper Hall

Juniper Hall (250 Oxford St.) is the oldest standing example of a Georgian villa in Australia. Completed in 1824, it was built by convict settler Robert Cooper, who made his fortune as a gin distiller and legendarily had 28 children. The residence was saved from demolition in the 1980s and is now restored to its former glory and used as offices.

Uniting Church and Parsonage

The **Uniting Church and Parsonage** (395 Oxford St., tel. 02/9331-2646, 10:30am Sun. service) was built in 1877 on the site of the first church building in Paddington. The pretty sandstone church and its outbuildings are a bustling center of worship and community events but are probably now best known for the Paddington Markets held here every Saturday.

Paddington Markets

Paddington Markets (Uniting Church grounds, 395 Oxford St., tel. 02/9331-2923, Sat. 10am-5pm in summer, 10am-4pm in winter), Sydney's longest-running community market, began in 1973 in the Paddington Uniting Church. The market was always a place for artists and designers to mingle and flog their wares. It is home to an eclectic range of stalls offering a wide array of Australian goods plus foods. Top-notch cuisine is widely available, and fresh juices, barbecue, freshly made soups, Thai food, and cakes and other baked goods are available for purchase. The market is home to a host of local artwork and creative outlets. Fashion, in particular, is widely displayed, and emerging designers sell their merchandise at bargain prices. The impressive selection of Australian-made goods parallels the creative talent found in the city of Paddington.

Paddington Public School

Paddington Public School (399-435 Oxford St.) is another one of the string of gorgeous heritage buildings lining Oxford Street and one of the oldest continuously operating schools in NSW. Built in the Romanesque Revival architectural style, it is at once imposing as well as homely. The school dates back to 1856, when it started with a portable building brought over from England, designed for 200 pupils. It quickly grew and by 1892 some 1,400 students attended classes in the school. The school is still regularly named one of the top primary schools in Sydney.

Centennial Park

A little farther on toward Bondi Junction from Paddington Public School is **Centennial Park** (Oxford St.). Originally a large natural catchment area of creeks, swamps, springs, sand dunes, and ponds fed by groundwater, it was traditionally home to the Gadi people. But with a growing population to feed, in 1811 Governor Lachlan Macquarie designated the area as the second Sydney Common, making use of it for grazing, lime burning, and timber clearing. Sir Henry Parks dedicated the area as Centennial Park in 1888, and it played a key role in the inauguration of the Australian Federation, held in the park in 1901.

Although originally designed as a

traditional Victorian-style park with formal gardens, ponds, statues, and wide avenues for horse carriages and buggies, it also has a wide variety of Australian flora and fauna, grasslands, and woodlands. Many sculptures, statues, and heritage buildings and structures dot the park's paths, but the emphasis today is on recreation, and you can go horse-riding, play sports, and rent bicycles to explore the park.

Fox Studios

The **Fox Studios** (38 Driver Ave., Moore Park, tel. 02/9383-4200, www.foxstudiosaustralia.com) were built on the former grounds of Sydney's Royal Easter Show, a grand event full of agricultural competitions (best pig sort of thing), animal experiences, sheep sheering, exhibitions of all kinds of agricultural implements and produce, and lots of fun. It is the largest event of its kind in Australia, the sixth largest in the world, and has taken place regularly starting in 1869. In 1998 the show moved to new grounds, leaving the vast space open for Fox Studios to move in, building a full-fledged studio complete with sound stages, exterior filming locations, costume department, catering, and everything else a major film might need. It's not open to the public, but films such as *The Great Gatsby, Wolverine, Australia, Superman, The Matrix, Babe,* and many others were filmed here.

THE NORTHERN SHORE

The northern shore is mostly residential, although there are a handful of attractions worth visiting and some great views to be had.

Kirribilli Point

Admiralty House (Kirribilli, www.theaustralianafund.org.au) is the Sydney residence of the governor-general of Australia. Built in 1842 as a single-story Georgian-style home, it was originally named Wotonga. From 1885 to 1913, the property was the residence of the admiral of the British Royal Navy's Australian Squadron, and its name was changed to Admiralty House. During this period a second story and stone colonnades were added. Since 1913 Admiralty House has been used on and off as a residence for the governor-general when in Sydney. The colonial-style house, with wrap-around verandas on both floors, arched colonnades, and French windows opening to the views across the harbor, no longer quite commands as imposing a plot of land as Kirribilli House but is still prime Sydney real estate.

Near Admiralty House on Kirribilli Point, **Kirribilli House** (Kirribilli, www.theaustralianafund.org.au) is positioned in probably the prime real estate position in all Sydney—overlooking the harbor, the bridge, and the opera house. Built in 1854, the twin-gabled, Gothic-style house is the official Sydney residence of the prime minister of Australia.

Note: Once a year is **Open Day,** during which several normally private residences and governmental buildings are open for the public to buy limited tickets to gain entrance and have a look around. This usually happens around September, but exact dates are only released just before the event. Entrance tickets are typically around $10 per site (tel. 02/9283-9567, www.theaustralianafund.org.au).

Nutcote

Nutcote (5 Wallaringa Ave., Neutral Bay, tel. 02/9953-4453, www.nutcote.org, Wed.-Thurs. 11am-3pm, adult $9, child $3.50, family $20) was the home of May Gibb, whose *The Complete Adventures of Snugglepot & Cuddlepie* is still today one of Australia's best-loved children's books. The author and illustrator (1877-1969) built Nutcote house and gardens with her husband in 1925, and she lived there for 44 years. Today it is the gardens that draw visitors. Sloping down to the shore, the gardens are a riot of colors, with an attractive mix of local and imported plants and trees. Have a look at the adorable book before you go and you will see exactly how and where May Gibb got her inspiration.

★ Taronga Zoo

Even if you don't generally like the idea of

The Northern Shore

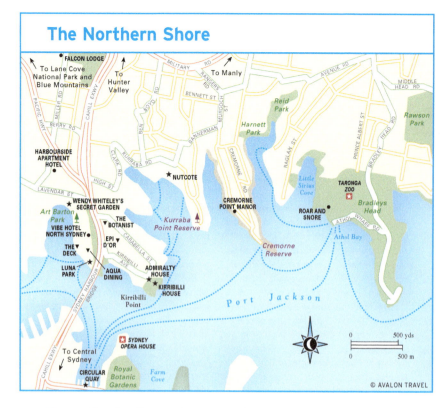

zoos, **Taronga Zoo** (Bradleys Head Rd., Mosman, tel. 02/9969-2777, www.taronga.org.au, daily 9am-5pm, May-Aug. closes at 4:30pm, adult $46, child $23, family $83-124) is a must-see in Australia. Undoubtedly the zoo with the best views in the world, overlooking the harbor, the bridge, the opera house, and the Sydney skyline, it is also arranged superbly to allow the animals plenty of space and make walking around a pleasant experience. Views are taken into consideration, and there are plenty of opportunities to get up close and personal with quite a few of the animals. Different sections specialize in African animals (with the giraffes having the best views in the house) or Australian animals, and there's even a farm where kids can hug a pet, learn about sheep shearing, meet the goats and pigs, and have plenty of fun. Encounters, feedings, and conservation talks are scheduled throughout the day, and there is a nighttime house where time is reversed so you can finally see all those nocturnal animals doing their thing. Inside, look out for the tiniest sugar gliders—tiny possums the size of a mouse, yet they can "float" between trees some 20 meters apart.

And even better? You can stay the night. See the website for details.

Wendy Whiteley's Secret Garden

Wendy Whiteley's Secret Garden (Lavender Bay) was created by the wife of the late Australian artist Brett Whiteley, after his death in 1992. Wendy channelled her grief and sorrow by transforming a previously neglected site into a secret garden full of sculptures, benches, and little hidden places, and continued to do so after the death of her only child, Arkie, from cancer. The ashes of Brett and Arkie are buried in the garden at an undisclosed location. Today the garden is open to everyone who is willing to find it, and is quite often used for blessing ceremonies and small weddings.

There are two ways to find the garden. The first option: Walk down from the North Sydney train station—aim for the Blue Street exit, turn right, and go up the steps toward Lavender Bay. Follow the road and then climb down the steps next to the little Indian Harbour Restaurant. On the left, the white house with the tower is the Whiteley House; the garden is just down a few steps also on the left. The second option: You can come from Lavender Bay, take the ferry to McMahons Point, walk left along the boardwalk in front of Luna Park, walk right under the arch and up steep steps and look for the house. It's a bit of a treasure hunt to find it, but it is a "secret garden," not found in many guides.

Step down from the garden through the railway bridge and walk along the **Art Barton Park,** a quirky display of miniature statues and sculptures celebrating the work of said Art Barton, who worked at Luna Park from 1937 to 1970, and who painted the scenes and created the huge smiling face that is the entrance to the park.

Luna Park

Dating back to the early 1930s, **Luna Park** (1 Olympic Dr, Milsons Point, tel. 02/9033-7676, www.lunaparksydney.com, hours vary, but generally weekdays 10am-6pm, weekends until 11pm) has not much changed over the years, offering good old-fashioned but nevertheless fun rides to kids of all ages, as well as food stalls, arcade games, slides, and excellent views. An Unlimited Rides Pass entitles you to unlimited rides for a full day. The cost of the pass depends on the height of the visitor: red (85-105 cm) $24.95, green (106-129 cm) $34.95, yellow (over 130 cm) $44.95. A single ride ticket is $10.

Lane Cove National Park

Some 10 kilometers north of Sydney, the 3.72-square-kilometer **Lane Cove National Park** (Lady Game Dr., Chatswood West, tel. 02/8448-0400, www.environment.nsw.gov.au, daily 9am-7pm during daylight savings, otherwise until 6pm, free) seems a million miles away from the bustling CBD. A pocket of bushland, this is a perfect place for walks or hiring a boat to meander along the peaceful

gondolas at Luna Park

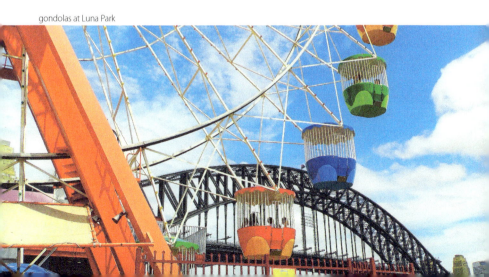

river. The **Lane Cove Boat Shed** (Riverside Drive North Ryde, 4.5 km inside the park, www.lanecoveboatshed.com.au, weekends 10am-5pm) hires out boats (pedal boat 30 minutes $25, single kayak 1 hour $30). Take a picnic, or simply bring a book and relax. On occasions such as fire danger or severe weather the park may have to close at short notice.

ISLAND HOPPING IN SYDNEY HARBOUR

Within Port Jackson, more commonly known as Sydney Harbour, are six islands, all of them managed by **National Parks of NSW** (www.nationalparks.nsw.gov.au). Further information on any of the islands is available from the **Sydney Harbour National Park Information Centre** in Cadman's Cottage (110 George St., The Rocks, tel. 02/9253-0888).

Cockatoo Island

Cockatoo Island is west of Sydney Harbour Bridge, next to its smaller neighbor, Spectacle Island, a Royal Australian Navy Armament depot that is not open to the public. Named after the ubiquitous sulphur-crested cockatoos that frequented the island when it was still called Waremah by the native Eora people, in the early 1800s Cockatoo Island became a penal establishment to alleviate overcrowding on Norfolk Island, which between 1788 and 1814 functioned as an extension of the penal settlement in NSW. It stayed a prison on and off, interspersed with naval shipbuilding and other naval activities until 1908. Shipbuilding continued until 1992, when most buildings were demolished and the island lay abandoned for a decade. The Sydney Harbour Federation Trust realized the historical importance of the island, and after extensive restoration work, Cockatoo Island opened to the public in 2007.

In 2010 Cockatoo Island was placed on the UNESCO World Heritage List. Now the island is a hot spot of major events, such as the Biennale of Sydney in 2014; recreational activities such as tennis, kayaking, and fishing; and historical tours around the restored buildings. **Audio tours** can be arranged at the visitors center for $5 each, or $8 shared between two. You can even stay the night, with accommodation provided in **luxury apartments** (from $240 per night) or at a **campground** (from $40), with unique views across the harbor. Check www.cockatooisland.gov.au for information and online booking. To get to Cockatoo Island, take the **Cockatoo Island ferry** from Circular Quay (Wharf F, weekdays every 30 minutes, weekends every 15 minutes, round-trip tickets $7 pp).

Rodd Island

Rodd Island, southwest of Cockatoo Island, is a small island, previously used as a biological research institute under instruction from Louis Pasteur, a dance studio in the late 1800s/early 1900s, and a U.S. Army base during World War II. Two pretty summer houses make this a favorite spot for weddings and parties. The only way to get there is by water taxi, such as **Sydney Cove Water Taxi** (tel. 04/1470-8020), which costs around $150 round-trip for up to eight passengers.

Goat Island

Goat Island, lying just off the inner-western suburb of Balmain to the west of the Sydney Harbour Bridge, was used as a home for convict work gangs and as a gunpowder storage depot in the 1800s. The Queen's Gunpowder Magazine, which stands on Goat Island, was built in the 1830s by convicts using sandstone quarried from the eastern side of the island. It was used to store explosives, and beside it stand barracks, a cooperage, and a kitchen. Later, Goat Island was the site of the first water police station and harbor fire brigade. Following this, the island served as a shipyard, and in more recent years it has been a location for filming and concerts.

A handful of historical buildings make a walking tour interesting, but the main reason to come would be a picnic on the lawn with the stunning view of the bridge and Sydney's CBD. There usually is very restricted access to the island, but in 2013, limitations were relaxed a little and a Captain Cook Cruises ferry was operational. At the time of writing, the ferry is still available from Circular Quay. If in doubt, guided **tours** can be booked via www.sydney.com.au, priced at $69, including ferry and guided walking tour, with a duration of around 2 hours 45 minutes.

Fort Denison

Fort Denison is a tiny fortified structure on an even tinier island just off the Sydney Opera House. After the First Fleet arrived in 1788, the island was informally known to locals as Pinchgut (a skinflint person who starves himself), as it was believed convicts were sentenced to weeks at a time isolated on the island with little bread and water. The fort features the only Martello Tower to be built in Australia, and the final one ever constructed in the British Empire.

Today, there is no chance to starve, with a **restaurant** (reservations tel. 02/9361-5208, around $30 per main) offering a varied menu of classic dishes and Australian specialties for lunch and dinner and probably the best views in the city. Bookings are essential for the daily 30-minute **tours** (tel. 02/9253-0888, Mon.-Tues. at 12:15pm and 2:30pm, Wed.-Sun. at 10:45am, 12:15pm, and 2:30pm) around the small island. To get there, either use a **Captain Cook Cruises ferry** (tel. 02/9206-1111, www.captaincook.com.au, prices depend on tours available) from Circular Quay and/or Darling Harbour or take a water taxi, which can be ordered individually from **Sydney Cove Water Taxi** (tel. 04/1470-8020, around $65 one way for two people).

Clark Island

Clark Island, just off Darling Point, was named after Lieutenant Ralph Clark, who back in the late 1700s cultivated this 0.9-hectare island as a vegetable garden. Today there is no longer a veggie patch, but the island is popular with walkers and picnickers. It's limited to 150 people per day, so you will need to prebook a visit. It is even possible to rent the entire island for a private function. Call tel. 02/9253-0888 to find out more. To get to Clark Island, take a water taxi, which can be ordered individually from **Sydney Cove Water Taxi** (tel. 04/1470-8020, around $80 one way for two people from Circular Quay).

Shark Island

Shark Island in Rose Bay is overlooked by some of Sydney's best real estate and in turn has amazing views of the entire harbor down to the opera house and bridge, with the CBD as backdrop. Now a pretty parkland island, it used to be a quarantine facility for animals and a naval storage depot. It was named not for the presence of sharks but, as legend has it, for its shape resembling a shark. The island is difficult to access, but **Captain Cook Cruises' "Hop On Hop Off" ferry** (www.captaincook.com.au, from $40) will stop at the jetty.

THE BEACHES

Australia does beaches very well and Sydney is no exception. There are beaches within the harbor, on its islands, and all along the Pacific Ocean. Many are within a mere 10 kilometers of the city center, most at the end of a straight bus connection from the city and all of them gorgeous, sandy, and inviting. Sydney's status as one of the most livable—and visitable—cities in the world is due to the proximity of city and beach lifestyle. There are many beaches—too many, except the most famous ones, to mention here. But these are so good that they will suffice in showing you what a surfers' paradise Sydney is, and to give you a chance to top up your tan and have a quick swim in the sea. If you can't make it out of town and want to combine sightseeing or brunch with a quick visit to the beach, try **Balmoral Beach** on the northern shore, where you can enjoy a leisurely brunch or lunch in the Bathers' Pavilion right on the beach.

★ Bondi Beach

Bondi, or Boondi (an Aboriginal word meaning "the noise of water breaking over rocks"), hardly needs an introduction—its fame has spread beyond Australia's shores. Bondi, on the southern shore, is the iconic surfer beach where the lifeguards ply their trade, pulling out unsuspecting swimmers who have underestimated the riptides or swallowed a little too much water while off their surfboards. But it's all good, and the popularity of this beach speaks for itself. In the summer and on the weekends it is sometimes difficult to see the sand between the people, but the beach is wide enough to accommodate everybody, and there are dedicated parts of the beach for surfers and swimmers. Get changed into your swimming costume at the beach pavilion, and head off to learn to surf or play beach ball or even beach volleyball.

One thing that is a must-do, even if it will take you away from the beach, is the **Bondi to Coogee coastal walk.** Start off in Bondi, to the right if you are facing the sea, and start to ascend past the iconic **Bondi Icebergs** (1 Notts Ave., tel. 02/9130-3120, daily 11am-late, adult $5.50, child $3.50, spectator $3), a swimming club that has been in place since 1929 and has the fantastic location overlooking the entire beach and bay, while allowing you to swim both in a pool and the sea. (How, you might ask? There is of course the pool, a neatly laned rectangle of green water, but it is built so close to the rocks that in regular intervals the natural waves from the ocean crash into the corner of the pool, offering some refreshment.)

To continue on the walk, simply follow the coastal route and you will walk past stunning coastal views, with regular stop-off points. Each year in and around October-November the **Sculpture by the Sea** festival (www.sculpturebythesea.com) displays sculptures all along this first stretch of the walk, offering modern art set off beautifully by the natural surroundings.

Have a brief drink at the beach café on the quaint little **Tamarama Beach,** then continue on to beautiful **Bronte Beach** (maybe stop for lunch) and past the Waverley Cemetery, with the best views to be had anywhere, then finish up at the great sandy expanse of **Coogee Beach.** The entire walk should take you around two hours to complete. It is some six kilometers long, and the difficulty level is easy to medium, but it does undulate from steep inclines to softer hills, and there are a few steps along the way. You'll be rewarded with some of the most amazing coastal scenery Australia has to offer. You can then either walk back or take the bus back into

Bondi Icebergs swimming pool on Bondi Beach

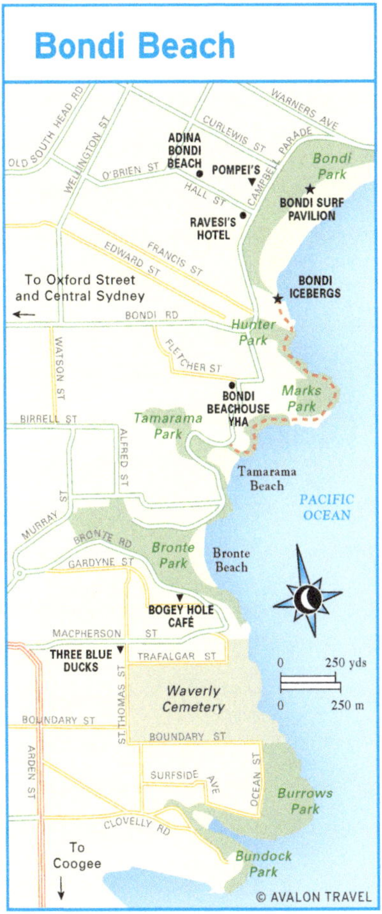

Bondi Beach

(Map of Bondi Beach area showing streets including Old South Head Rd, Wellington St, O'Brien St, Hall St, Francis St, Edward St, Bondi Rd, Fletcher St, Birrell St, Watson St, Alfred St, Murray St, Bronte Rd, Gardyne St, Macpherson St, Trafalgar St, St Thomas St, Boundary St, Surfside Ave, Ocean St, Clovelly Rd, Arden St, Warners Ave, Curlewis St, Campbell Parade; landmarks including Adina Bondi Beach, Pompei's, Ravesi's Hotel, Bondi Surf Pavilion, Bondi Park, Bondi Icebergs, Hunter Park, Bondi Beachouse YHA, Marks Park, Tamarama Park, Tamarama Beach, Bronte Park, Bronte Beach, Bogey Hole Café, Three Blue Ducks, Waverly Cemetery, Burrows Park, Bundock Park; with arrows To Oxford Street and Central Sydney, and To Coogee; Pacific Ocean to east. © AVALON TRAVEL)

Sydney from Coogee. Be sure to bring some water and sunscreen.

Manly

Many say that Manly on the northern shore is a better beach than Bondi, but opinions are divided, and there is no right or wrong. Where Bondi is a beautiful curved beach in a bay setting with its village setting behind it, Manly is straighter and directly on the open ocean with tall Norfolk Island pine trees lining the beach. Both are stunning, with plenty of white sand, great surfing and swimming, and the beach esplanades offering everything from an ice cream to a glass of cold beer.

Manly stretches for some two kilometers, with beaches at either end, each offering a little walk and another scenic bay: **Queenscliff Beach** to the north just across the creek and little **Shelly Beach** to the south. If you are after a harder walk, a hike from Manly toward Sydney along the coastline of the harbor, the **Manly to Spit Bridge Walk,** offers one of the most beautiful walks in Sydney, but this is a three- to four-hour trek, which you can either take on in its entirety or split into smaller sections. Some of the section through the **Sydney Harbour National Park** can be quite steep and hard, whereas others are an easy saunter. Bus 143/144 follows roughly the same route, so you can catch that back at any time. For details of the various sections of the walk, have a look at www.wildwalks.com to plan ahead.

If jazz and beach are your perfect combination, then the annual **Manly Jazz** festival is for you. Having been a fixed occasion on the calendar since 1977, Manly Jazz has a rich history of dishing up some of the best live jazz performances from across Australia and around the world. Taking place usually over a long October weekend, this is an iconic event on the Australian music scene and is firmly positioned as Sydney's biggest celebration of all things jazz. Check the dates at www.manly.nsw.gov.au before you go.

Manly does not only beach and music, but also beach and art. Since 1994, the **Manly Arts Festival** (www.manlyartsfestival.com.au) has brought together art as diverse as the ocean and sky over a long weekend in September. From photography competitions and fine art exhibitions to dance demonstrations and drawing workshops, there are events to cater to all tastes.

To have a look past the beach and under the waves, check out **Manly Sea Life Sanctuary** (West Esplanade, Manly, tel. 02/8251-7877, www.manlysealifesanctuary.com.au, daily 10am-5:30pm, from adult $16.80, child $8.40, family $47). This is a lovely aquarium-cum-rescue center where the staff not only successfully breed animals in captivity, but also

nurture sick wild animals back to health before releasing them again. There is a colony of little penguins (*Eudyptula minor*), an exhibit of everything that swims in Sydney Harbour (from sea horses to octopus to sharks), and an underwater shark tunnel. You can even jump into the aquarium and go for a shark dive (from $155 for a certified dive, $216 for an introductory dive, overall length 2.5 hours).

DAY TOURS
Walking Tours

The self-guided **City of Sydney's historical walking tours** (pick up a detailed map at any visitors center or print a PDF from www.cityofsydney.nsw.gov.au) include a tour of commercial and retail Sydney that is a must for lovers of architecture and shopping. The CBD is brimming with historic buildings, be they of Victorian or Art Deco heritage. Many either used to be old department stores or have evolved into modern shopping complexes in old shells. Explore the history of retail along Pitt Street and Martin Place, including the magnificent Queen Victoria Building, the Strand Arcade, and the Grace Hotel.

Explore Sydney's spooky side with **Ghost Tours** (meet outside Cadman's Cottage, opposite the Orient Hotel, 110 George St., The Rocks, tel. 02/9241-1283, www.ghosttours.

com.au, Apr.-Sept. daily 6:45pm, Oct.-March daily 7:45pm, 2 hours, $42). Hear true stories about murder, suicide, hangings, hauntings, recent ghost sightings, and strange phenomena, while you walk along through the cobblestone lanes of the historic Rocks. Special Halloween tours are also available. The tours are geared toward adults, though between Sunday and Thursday 13- to 17-year-olds may attend with a paying adult ($33 per teen). Teenagers cannot attend on Friday and Saturday evenings.

A pub crawl through The Rocks with **Sydney Pub Tours** (meet inside the Mercantile Hotel, 25 George St., The Rocks, tel. 04/1966-9832, www.sydneypubtours.com, Mon.-Fri. 6pm-9:30pm, $125 including drinks and dinner, must be over 18) will show you the Australian pub culture while informing you about the colonial history of the old pubs and the area. Stop at five historic pubs, get a complimentary wine/beer/soft drink at each location, have dinner in one location, get access behind the scenes, learn plenty of information, and have fun along the way.

Two Feet & a Heartbeat (tel. 1800/459-388, www.twofeet.com.au) offers walking tour options. The "Kings Cross Crime and Passion Tour" (from the Coke sign, corner William St. and Darlinghurst Rd., daily at 6pm, 2 hours, $40) explores the seedy and violent history of Kings Cross of the 1920s and 1930s; hear stories and see locations of murders, prostitution, gambling, and romance and try to imagine what it was like to live in this part of town in those darker times. Roughly following the Tank Stream, "Sydney with Conviction" (from Booking Centre, Wharf 6, Circular Quay, daily at 10am, 2 hours, $40) takes in the Sydney Harbour Bridge, The Rocks, Sydney Opera House, and the sights along the old Tank Stream route to Hyde Park.

I'm Free (Town Hall Square, 483 George St., CBD, www.imfree.com.au) offers free walking tours of Sydney: "Sydney Sights" (starting from the anchor on the Town Hall Square on George St., daily 10:30am and 2:30pm, 2.5-3 hours, free) heads up George Street, taking in sights such as Sydney Tower, the Talking Dog, Hyde Park Barracks, Martin Place, Sydney Opera House, and The Rocks. The tour ends at Circular Quay. "The Rocks" (meet in front of Cadman's Cottage, Circular Quay, daily 6pm, 1.5 hours, free) explores that area where Sydney began, including the lanes, Susannah Place, and Observatory Hill. You'll hear stories about the Rum Rebellion, Australia's largest bank robbery, evil murders, and the checkered history of the area.

The Rocks Dreaming Aboriginal Tour (from Cadman's Cottage, 110 George St., Circular Quay, tel. 02/8273-0000, www.therocks.com/therocksdreamingbookings, daily 10:30am, 1.5 hours, adult $42, child $32, children under 8 free) was developed by Margret Campbell, a Dunghutti-Jerrinjah woman, and is led by Aboriginal guides who have her permission to share her cultural knowledge. You will learn about the country before the settlers, hear the local language, experience cultural traditions, and even get your hands dirty with some ochre painting. Did you know that the Aboriginals were classed under "flora and fauna," not people, until 1967?

If you are interested in water features, be it fountains, following the old Tank Stream, drinking fountains, sewers, or even old-fashioned toilets, the self-guided **Walk on Water** (pick up a detailed map at any visitors center or print a PDF from www.cityofsydney.nsw.gov.au) is a quirky walk that you can pick up from anywhere and follow at your leisure, exploring a different side of Sydney's history.

Day Trips in and around Sydney

Sydney Boutique Tours (7 Campbell St., Artamon, tel. 02/9436-1333, www.sydneyboutiquetours.com.au, adult $250, child under 14 years $229) offers a boutique wildlife tour to the Southern Highlands, pristine bushland where Australia's iconic wildlife (such as kangaroos, wallabies, koalas, and emus) lives without the need for zoos or fences—just a 90-minute drive outside Sydney. This tour leaves at noon and does not return until later in the evening to ensure you have the chance to spot some of the nocturnal animals, such as possums and wombats. Travel in a small group with your own naturalist guide in a four-wheel-drive vehicle, stopping for lunch or afternoon tea and dinner while on "safari."

Take a tour to Canberra, Australia's capital city, with **Down Under Day Tours** (tel. 02/9251-7069, www.downunderdaytours.com.au, Mon., Wed., and Fri., hotel pickup around 7am, returning at 9pm, adult $125, child $63). You'll see the New and Old Parliaments, the Aboriginal embassy, the Australia War Memorial, the National Museum of Australia, Lake Burley Griffin, and Mount Ainslie. Tour cost includes a guided tour of parliament, entry to the war memorial, and entry to either the national gallery or the national museum.

Wachtl Australia (62/209 Harris St., Pyrmont, tel. 04/1208-6034, www.wachtlaustralia.com.au, from $198) offers a tour to Jervis Bay, where you can swim, go on dolphin trips, or simply relax and enjoy the unspoiled wilderness surroundings of Booderee National Park. Drive out of the city southward, and along the way see Botany Bay, where the first settlers arrived but did not stay; visit the impressive blowhole at Kiama; and spend some time on the pristine Hyams Beach, where you will hopefully be able to spot dolphins and maybe even humpback whales. A 10-hour round-trip, this tour gives you another impression of what's around the city.

EcoTreasures (tel. 04/1512-1648, http://ecotreasures.com.au, adult $145, child $99, hotel pickup 8am, around 5.5 hours, lunch included) takes you north of the city to explore Australia's Aboriginal heritage on the "Northern Beaches Cultural Heritage Tour." Walk with an expert cultural guide through Ku-ring-gai National Park and learn about the local peoples' art, culture, and traditions. Discuss Australia's native wildlife and ecosystems, search for tracks, and learn about bush tucker; then drive to West Head, which is home to culturally significant Aboriginal sites, including rock engravings, hand stencils, and midden sites.

Find the true essence of Australia in the rural Outback on the "Tobruk Sheep Station Outback Experience" tour offered by **Sightseeing** (tel. 1300/655-965, www.australiasightseeing.com, adult $149, child $75, around 6.5 hours). You will drive through NSW to a traditional farm, where you can watch the stockmen muster sheep and shear them, eat the typical "damper" (the soda bread prepared by campers in the Outback around a campfire), and maybe even try your hand at shearing or cracking a whip. Lunch is a typical steak followed by a lamington cake, and the experience feels a million miles away from modern Sydney. The return journey takes you past the majestic Hawkesbury River and through the Blue Mountains.

Looking for more than just a one-day trip? **Aussie Farmstay and Bush Adventures** (tel. 02/9660-3245, www.aussiebushadventures.com, adult $1,010, child $640) offers a four-day tour into the bush of Australia, experiencing the country and its ingrained traditions on a varied farm stay. On the way out of Sydney, you will visit the Koala Park Sanctuary and travel through the Blue Mountains to Mudgee for a wine tasting; the next day you will get into sheep shearing, bush craft, enjoying Australian bush tucker (food traditionally eaten and prepared by the Aboriginal peoples) around a campfire, and learning about the stars in the southern hemisphere sky. On day three, visit the country town of Canowindra, a fossil museum, and the Abercrombie Caves. Stay in the Megalong Valley in a log cabin. On day four you'll go horseback riding in the Jamison Valley, visit the Scenic Railway in Katoomba, and see Aboriginal rock art before heading back. All accommodations, meals, and activities are included.

Sports and Recreation

GARDENS AND PARKS
Ku-ring-gai Wildflower Garden
Ku-ring-gai Wildflower Garden (420 Mona Vale Rd., St. Ives, tel. 02/9424-0353, www.kmc.nsw.gov.au/kwg, daily 8am-5pm, free) is a mix of traditional bush land, heathland, fern tree gullies, ponds, and waterfalls spread across 123 hectares. Within the garden visitors can choose from a range of public access walking tracks, including the accessible Senses Track (15 minutes) or the more challenging Mueller Track (2 hours). Amenities include picnic areas with barbecues (some available for hire), on-site parking, toilet facilities, and a children's playground.

Nielsen Park
Found along the Rose Bay to Watsons Bay walk, **Nielsen Park** (Greycliffe Ave., Vaucluse, tel. 02/9253-0888, www.nationalparks.nsw.gov.au, daily sunrise-sunset but may close occasionally due to fire risk or severe weather, free) is part of the Sydney Harbour National Park, with stunning vistas across Sydney Harbour. It's a comfortable mix of open space and shady reserves, plus it features one of inner Sydney's best family beaches, Shark Beach, which is a great spot for snorkeling and swimming within the safe shark net. Amenities include a kiosk, toilet facilities, picnic tables with barbecues, and drinking water fountains.

Paddington Reservoir Gardens
The Paddington reservoir was a vital source of water for Sydney's rapidly growing population in the 19th century but eventually ceased supplying water in 1899. The site was neglected and fell into disuse until it was heritage-listed by the state and reinvented. Now an award-winning garden with parts of the original brickwork and timber and iron framework restored and incorporated in the design, **Paddington Reservoir Gardens** (251-255 Oxford St., tel. 02/9265-9333, daily sunrise-sunset, free) is an intriguing mix of ancient Roman-style baths and immaculate European gardens. This is a small secluded park, not necessarily a walking park, but perfect for a coffee and a book.

BIKING
Take in Sydney's historic sights and cycle across the Sydney Harbour Bridge with an experienced guide. There are several tours available with **Viator** (www.viator.com), ranging from a four-hour classic tour around all the main sights to a briefer highlight tour for 2.5 hours, as well as a Sydney Harbour Bridge ride (5 hours) and the Manly Beach sunset tour, which includes a ferry ride (4 hours, from $99 pp).

Life's an Adventure (tel. 02/9913-8939, www.lifesanadventure.com.au) also offers tour options. Bike around **Garigal National Park** (meet at P'Neenies Cafe, 6/5 Yulong Ave., Terrey Hills, hotel pickup $18, half day $145 pp, 10am-3:30pm), exploring the great trails. Or take a day trip to the **Blue Mountains** (hotel pickup from 7am or meet in Katoomba at 9:30am, finish 3:30pm, $185 pp, save $20 on Tues.). This is a fantastic guided mountain biking ride to Narrow Neck near Katoomba in the Blue Mountains, a plateau that stretches out into the wilderness dividing the Jamison and Megalong Valleys. The track provides a well-maintained undulating ride with four steep climbs and a couple of short, steep gullies, and breathtaking views throughout.

If you want to go it alone and just get some exercise in for a couple of hours, why not hire a bike in Centennial Park? You can go along the paths shared with pedestrians or the dedicated cycle paths, such as the Grand Drive, a 3.8-kilometer dedicated cycle lane. Rent bicycles from **Centennial Park Cycles** (50 Clovelly Rd., Randwick, tel. 02/9398-5027,

Sydney for Kids

- At the **Australian Museum** (6 College St., CBD, tel. 02/9320-6000, www.australianmuseum.net.au, daily 9:30am-5pm, adult $12, child 5-15 $6, family $30), you can get X-ray vision in the Hall of Bones, where you see the skeletons of people and lots of animals, including bats and even a snake.

- Bounce yourself happy at **Flipout Trampolines** (80 Mulgoa Rd., Penrith, www.flipout.net.au, Sun.-Thurs. 9am-10pm, Fri.-Sat. 9am-midnight, $10 for 30 minutes, $14 for 60 minutes).

- Cable cars and the world's steepest train rides are on offer at **Scenic World** (1 Violet St., Katoomba, tel. 02/4780-0200, www.scenicworld.com.au, daily 9am-5pm, adult $35, child 4-13 $18, family $88) in the Blue Mountains.

- Dodgems, roller coasters, and cotton candy are part of the all-day-long limitless fun at **Luna Park** (1 Olympic Dr, Milsons Point, tel. 02/9033-7676, www.lunaparksydney.com, hours vary, generally weekdays 10am-6pm during week, weekends until 11pm).

- Eat pancakes in all flavors, savory and sweet, in stacks and solo, at **Pancakes on the Rocks** (4 Hickson Rd., The Rocks, tel. 02/9247-6371, www.pancakesontherocks.com.au, daily 24 hours).

- Fly a kite at the **Bondi Beach Festival of the Winds** (www.waverly.nsw.gov.au, dates TBA, usually one Sunday in mid-September). Once a year there is an amazing display of kites in all shapes and sizes.

- Get your skates (and skateboards and BMX) on at the **Monster Skatepark** at Sydney Olympic Park (Grand Parade, Sydney Olympic Park, tel. 02/9763-7359, www.monsterpark.com.au, daily 9am-10pm, one-hour lesson from $30 including equipment).

- Hang out with Simba, Timon, and Pumba at *The Lion King*, the musical showing at Sydney's **Capitol Theatre** (13 Campbell St., Haymarket, tel. 1300/558-878, http://capitoltheatre.com.au, tickets from $50).

- Interested in science and looking for awesome cool toys, games, and experiments? Head to **Terrific Scientific** (51 Booth St., Annandale, tel. 02/9692-9206, www.terrificscientific.com.au, daily 10am-5:30pm).

- Join the fun at the newest water park in Sydney. There are countless slides, pipes and tipping buckets-of-fun for the whole family at **Wet'n'Wild** (427 Reservoir Rd., tel. 13/33-86, www.wetnwildsydney.com.au, summer daily 10am-5pm, from $54.99 for a day pass).

- **Koala Park Sanctuary** (84 Castle Hill Rd., West Pennant Hills, tel. 02/9484-3141, www.koalapark.com.au, daily 9am-5pm, adult $27, child $15) in the north of Sydney has koalas galore. Also meet kangaroos, dingoes, wombats, echidnas, emus, wallabies, and a large collection of birds in native bushland.

- Learn to surf at Bondi Beach. **Let's Go Surfing** (http://letsgosurfing.com.au, from $95 for 2-hour lesson) offers classes for beginners and near pros, as well as paddle boarding.

- Merrily go round on an old-fashioned carousel with beautiful horses, right next to the **Darling Harbour Playground** (www.darlingquarter.com/play). Other features include a giant 3-D swing, an Octanet, diggers, and messy water games.

- Need presents for friends back home? Get unusual souvenirs and toys at the **Australian**

Geographic Store (Westfield Bondi Junction, 500 Oxford St., Bondi Junction, tel. 02/9257-0060, http://shop.australiangeographic.com.au, Mon.-Wed. and Sat. 9:30am-6pm, Thurs. 9:30am-9pm, Fri. 9:30am-7pm). There are dinosaur eggs, magic kits, cuddly koalas, and more.

- Observe the sharks and the giant Japanese spider crab, which reaches 3.5 meters claw to claw, at **Sea Life Sydney Aquarium** (Aquarium Wharf/1-5 Wheat Rd., Darling Harbour, tel. 02/9333-9288, www.sydneyaquarium.com.au, daily 9am-8pm, last admission at 7pm, adult $26, child $16, family $65 if booked online).

- Pop into **Rip Curl** (98/100 The Corso, Manly) for some authentic Australian surfing gear.

- Question science, conduct some experiments, and find out for yourself at the **Powerhouse Museum** (500 Harris St., Ultimo, tel. 02/9217-0111, www.powerhousemuseum.com, daily 10am-5pm, adult $12, child $6, family $30).

- Reach to the stars at the **Sydney Observatory** (Watson Rd., Observatory Hill, tel. 02/9921-3485, www.sydneyobservatory.com.au), where night tours include a 3-D space session and you get to look at the sky through a gigantic telescope.

- Ships ahoy. Climb the mast on a tall ship in the harbor and get the best view of them all on a family pirate cruise with **Sydney Harbour Tall Ships** (tel. 02/8243-7961, www.sydneytallships.com.au, family pirate cruises $243 for family, mast climbing from 9 years old).

- Take the train along Darling Harbour. The little **People Mover** takes you from the Australian National Maritime Museum (2 Martin St.) past the playground to the Sea Life Sydney Aquarium and beyond, all for $5 adult, $4 child. It makes several stops all around the harbor basin.

- Upside down climbing and various rope challenges allow you to channel your inner Spiderman at Blaxland Riverside Park's **Urban Jungle Adventure Park** (Sydney Olympic Park Aquatic Centre, Olympic Blvd., Wentworth Point, tel. 02/9905-2559, www.urban-jungle.net.au, weekends 9:30am-6pm, weekdays by appointment only, $35 pp).

- Visit the red carpet at **Madame Tussauds** (Aquarium Wharf, 1-5 Wheat Rd., Darling Harbour, tel. 02/9333-9240, www.madametussauds.com/sydney, daily 9am-8pm, last admission at 7pm, adult $40, child $28, family $136, save 30% online), mingle with the stars, and get yourself an Oscar.

- What do will.i.am and Michael Jackson have in common? They left some of their stuff at the **Hard Rock Café** (Harbourside Centre, Level 2/2-10, Darling Dr., tel. 02/9280-0077, www.hardrock.com, Mon.-Fri. noon-late, Sat.-Sun. 11:30am-late, burger and fries $20) on Darling Harbour.

- Xmas displays at **Myer** (436 George St.) and **David Jones** (86-108 Castlereagh St.) in the CBD: If you happen to be in Sydney between late November and Christmas, don't miss the magical window displays at these two department stores.

- Yeehaw! Go horse riding in **Centennial Park** (www.centennialparklands.com.au, Sat.-Sun. 10am-2pm, pony rides child 2-11, $15).

- Zzzs at the zoo. Grab some Zzzs with the lions at **Taronga Zoo** (Bradleys Head Rd., Mosman, tel. 02/9969-2777, www.taronga.org.au, daily 9am-5pm, May-Aug. closes at 4:30pm, adult $44, child $22, family $270). Camp in the zoo and meet some animals behind the scenes.

daily 8:30am-5:30pm, children's bike from $10/hour, adult road bike from $20/hour).

HIKING

Harbour Walk (meet at Wharf 4, Circular Quay, tel. 04/0496-8968, daily 9am, from $89 pp, discounts for children) is an all-day walking tour with ferry rides to the starting point and returning. Take the ferry to Rose Bay, walk for around 3.5 hours at a leisurely pace along the coastline of the harbor, past Sydney Harbour National Park, along the bays to the prestigious suburb of Vaucluse. Have tea along the way, then fish and chips for lunch at Watsons Bay, and return to Circular Quay by ferry.

The walking enthusiasts at **Sydney Coast Walks** (tel. 02/8521-7423, www.sydneycoastwalks.com.au, from $75) know the best walks in and around Sydney's coast and offer half-, full- and two-day treks showing you the best of the scenery, bush, and national parks. They take out groups of like-minded people on a variety of walks catering to all fitness levels, and also offer personalized tours. Try the "Marley Walking Tour" (adult $145, child $135)—you'll get picked up at around 7am from your hotel and enjoy a roughly seven-hour walk through national parkland, with coastal views, cave exploration, wildlife sightings, and viewing Aboriginal engravings on the sandstone. Lunch is provided (and carried!), and you'll also enjoy a ferry round-trip.

Short Walks (http://short-walks.com.au) is a great website that allows you to search for walks according to location or duration. There are plenty of hikes in and around Sydney and New South Wales, including the Blue Mountains and the Southern Highlands, both of which offer a huge variety of walks. Each walk gives you an idea of difficulty level, duration, and length, and a reasonably detailed map, plus a weather forecast.

SNORKELING AND DIVING

Even though it is a harbor, there are more species of fish in Sydney Harbour than in the entire Mediterranean. For example, did you know there are numerous different species of seahorse found in the harbor? **EcoTreasures** (Q Station Wharf, Quarantine Beach, Manly, tel. 04/1512-1648, http://ecotreasures.com.au, group tours from adult $55, child $35) takes you out into the harbor to discover the myriad marine life. The 90-minute tour includes a marine eco talk, wet suits, noodles, snorkeling gear, and a guide.

If you want to go deeper, there is always scuba diving. **Pro Dive Experience** (169 Pittwater Rd., Manly, tel. 02/9977-5966, and 27 Alfred St., Coogee, tel. 02/8116-1199, www.prodive.com.au, from $69, including equipment) organizes shore and open-water dives, including night dives. They also offer a weekend openwater course for beginners (from $499) and advanced courses at two sites in Sydney (from $299).

Dive Centre Manly (10 Belgrave St., Manly, tel. 02/9977-4355, www.divesydney.com.au, from $95 one dive, $125 for two shore dives, including equipment) offers shore dives at Shelley Beach, where sightings of wobbegongs (carpet sharks) are common, and at other nearby sites that are not deep and are ideal for beginners. Boat dives include a shark dive to see gray nurse sharks, the South Head Sponge Gardens, and the Gap Cave, which offers a great variety of local fish, sponges, and underwater geology.

SURFING

If you would like to get into the surf culture, then Sydney is one of the best spots in Australia to try your hand at this sport. Both **Bondi Beach** and **Manly Beach** are world-renowned for all-year-round waves that lend themselves to world-class surfing. There are plenty of other beaches around and outside Sydney, but there you will have to bring your own gear and know where you are going and what you are doing. If you need to hire your equipment and are looking for a lesson or two, Bondi and Manly are the perfect spots to do both. The schools also hire out boards if you are already accomplished. At **Manly**

Beach Hire (www.manlybeachhire.com.au), directly on the sand, you can hire a surf- or bodyboard from $10 per hour; in Bondi Beach, **Let's Go Surfing** (http://letsgosurfing.com.au, 128 Ramsgate Ave., North Bondi, tel. 02/9365-1800) hires out surfboards from $20 per hour.

Let's Go Surfing also offers the "Bondi Surf Experience" (from $99), great for beginners or those needing to refresh their skills. It's a two-hour lesson on Australia's most famous beach, and you'll be in a small group. Or get a private lesson ($140/hour, with board, wet suit, and sunblock included) with a professional, either learning the basics or improving on the skills you have.

Manly Surf School (North Styne, Manly, tel. 02/9932-7000, http://manlysurfschool.com.au, tours from $120, lessons from $70 adult, $55 child) offers not only lessons for beginners and advanced surfers, but a day-long "Surf Tour." Be picked up at 9:30am in the city, learn about surfing (including the history and local importance), then drive to one of the nearby northern beaches for a 90-minute lesson. Have a typical Aussie pie for lunch, another lesson, and head back around 4pm. They also do paddleboard lessons (from $35, all gear included).

KAYAKING

Life's an Adventure (tel. 02/9913-8939, www.lifesanadventure.com.au) gives you a chance to watch Sydney wake up during a great morning kayak tour through Sydney Harbour (Woollahra Sailing Club, Vickery Ave., Rose Bay, adult $99 pp, child 8-16 years $65, pickup from hotel $10). Go past the opera house and the bridge, and explore the coves around the inner harbor. Meet with your guide at Rose Bay at 7am, tour the harbor, and be back by 9:30am, ready for a day's sightseeing. Another option is the biking, hiking, and kayaking experience (Craig Avenue Boat ramp, Little Manly Beach, Manly, 9:30am-5pm, adult $199, child 10-16 $179, save $20 pp on Mon.). For a sporting day out taking in the northern beaches, this adventure involves an entire day of biking, hiking, and kayaking. Start with cycling to Manly's beautiful North Head (the northern end of the entrance from the Pacific Ocean into Sydney Harbour), exploring the natural beauty and military history of the North Head national park. You then kayak around the secluded sandy coves and oceanic waters of Manly, stopping for lunch on a remote picturesque beach not accessible by road. Finish the day with a guided walk from Manly to The Spit, a point of coast

sailing yachts in Sydney Harbour

jutting out into the harbor, along the dramatic coastline and rugged bushland of the Sydney Harbour National Park, complete with photo opportunities and great views.

Natural Wanders (Milsons Point, tel. 04/2722-5072, www.naturalwanders.com.au, from $120 pp including photographs) offers custom **VIP Paddle** tours, which start early on weekdays, and you can suggest a route, the difficulty of the tour, and length. The "Bridge Paddle" route is a possibility for beginners on these trips, while on weekends this is for experienced sea kayakers only. Starting off at Lavender Bay on the north side of the Sydney Harbour Bridge, the Bridge Paddle takes you under the bridge, past Kirribilli Point opposite the opera house, paddling into bays and along beaches and past a bushland setting, giving you a whole new perspective of the harbor. This is quite an adventurous paddle combined with stunning scenic views, and will put your paddling skills to good use as well as improve your knowledge of Sydney's northern shore. Total distance is around 14 kilometers, and as tours are small and private, the timing can be set around your schedule and abilities.

SAILING

Bareboat Yacht Charter (yachts moored at d'Albora Marina, Rushcutters, tel. 02/9327-1166, www.eastsail.com.au, contact for charter prices) has a selection of yachts available for bareboat sailing charter on Sydney Harbour, including Beneteau 33.7, 40.7, First 40, Oceanis 40, Dufour 335, and Sydney 36 yachts. All come with well-equipped galley with gas oven, crockery and cutlery, fridge/icebox, private bathroom with hot water, CD stereo with iPod jack, and full safety inventory. You can also day-charter skippered private yachts, which come with a crew and hostess upon request, or join a "Morning Adventure Sail" (10am-12:30pm, adult $119, child $89, minimum of four adults) or a "Sunset Cruise" (6pm-8pm, $596 for four guests, including drinks and snacks).

Sydney by Sail (Festival Pontoon, National Maritime Museum, Darling Harbour, tel. 02/9280-1110, www.sydneybysail.com.au, $1,395 per couple) offers a romantic overnight sailing experience on a Hunter 39 yacht. Set off from Darling Harbour, sail around Sydney Harbour taking in the sights and early sunset, and then anchor for the night. The hired skipper will leave you on our own, securely anchored. Dinner and breakfast are provided and in the morning the skipper will return you to Sydney.

Want to sail on an Americas Cup Yacht? **Adrenalin** (20 Burton St., Darlinghurst, tel. 1300/791-793, www.adrenalin.com.au, from $79) will take you on a 2.5-hour cruise on the 75-foot racing yacht. It departs King Street Wharf, Darling Harbour and then takes in the sights and thrills of Sydney Harbour, with an experienced crew allowing you to pitch in along the journey. There are usually up to 30 guests, and only selected dates are available.

CRUISES AND RIDES

Sydney Harbour Tall Ships cruises (book at Kiosk 3, Wharf 5, Circular Quay, tel. 02/8243-7961, www.sydneytallships.com.au, from adult $99, child $45) depart from Campbell's Cove, The Rocks. They give you an opportunity to go out into the harbor on a tall ship—not quite the size of ship the first settlers came on, but more authentic than a modern motor yacht any day. Lounge around on the deck, or maybe climb up into the mast to get an even better view and savor the history. When the sails are set and you look back into the harbor, you'll get a much better feeling for how it must have been in the early days. On the "Convicts, Castles & Champagne Tour" (Thurs.-Mon. at 1pm, additional cruises weekends 11:30am and 2:30pm, 2.75 hours, adult $89, child $39), you'll cruise along the harbor, stop off at Goat Island, tour the 1800s gunpowder magazine, learn about convict history, and sail past some of Sydney's best real estate and the government houses, while enjoying an open bar, including free local bubbles. There are even special "Family Pirate Tours" (usually 1.5 hours long; departure times and dates vary seasonally and according to school

Sydney Harbour Tall Ships cruise

holidays), or you can opt for the more sophisticated "Wine and Canapés Tour" at sunset (3 hours, adults only, $149 includes finger foods and unlimited wine, beer, and soft drinks; mast climb $25).

Captain Cook Cruises (tel. 02/9206-1111, www.captaincook.com.au) offers a "Coffee Cruise" (departs Jetty 6, Circular Quay, daily 10am and 2:15pm, 2 hours, adult $39, child $10) that runs along the harbor, taking in all the sights, islands, beaches, cliffs, and real estate on the waterfront, while you enjoy morning or afternoon tea and coffee and listen to the personalized commentary. Captain Cook also offers "Hop On Hop Off" (from adult $45, child $24, family $90), a 24-hour pass allowing unlimited access to the hop-on, hop-off ferry that takes in eight main sights on the harbor, including Taronga Zoo, Fort Denison, Shark Island, Manly, Luna Park, and others. You can pay extra and have entrance fees to other sights, such as the Sea Life Sydney Aquarium, Madame Tussauds, Wild Life Sydney Zoo, Sydney Tower Eye, Fort Denison, and Shark Island included in the price. Prices vary according to how many attractions you opt for. On the "Dinner Cruise" (departs Jetty 6, Circular Quay, or Jetty 1, King Street Wharf, Darling Harbour, daily 7pm, 2.5-3 hours, from $89, adults only), you'll enjoy sparkling nighttime Sydney views from the water during a three-course contemporary Australian à la carte dinner with live music and dancing.

TourChief (tel. 02/8296-7233, www.tourchief.com) offers a simple harbor sightseeing cruise (code AUS1511; departs daily every two hours from the following: Darling Harbour, Circular Quay, Taronga Zoo, Watsons Bay, Manly, Q Station, Milson's Point, two hours, adult $28, child $15, family $71) with running commentary, taking in all the sights along the harbor from the bridge to the opera house, going past some of the many islands and allowing you to enjoy the city skyline and unusual perspective of sights from the water.

See Sydney Harbour at breakneck speeds on a powerful jet boat with **OzJetBoating** (depart from the east side of Circular Quay, tel. 02/9808-3700, www.ozjetboating.com, hourly departures daily 11am-4pm, 30 minutes, adult $70, child $45, family $195). Get wet (coveralls provided) and thrilled while splashing along past the opera house to Shark Island, Taronga Zoo, and the Sydney Harbour Bridge.

To get a whole new perspective of Sydney and the scenic harbor, try flying over it with **Sydney by Seaplane** (tel. 02/9974-1455, www.sydneybyseaplane.com, daily 7am-10pm, departures from Rose Bay). Flights include a 15-minute trip (from $185 pp) across the bridge and opera house to Manly and Bondi Beach, as well as dinner flights (from $365 not including dinner and drinks), where the plane takes you to the northern beaches or the Hawkesbury River, drops you off for a romantic dinner, and then flies you back home. Alternatively, opt for the "Gourmet Beach Picnic with Champagne" (from $890 pp, 3.5 hours, food and drinks included).

WHALE-WATCHING

The whale-watching season along NSW's east coast runs from May to November, and humpback and southern right whales migrate from the Antarctic up to the Great Barrier Reef for breeding. More than 50 percent of the planet's cetaceans, whales, dolphins, and porpoises can be found in Australia, with nine species of baleen whales and 36 species of toothed whales living in the local waters. Thousands of whales swim past, and sometimes into, Sydney Harbour, and there are plenty of cruises to take advantage of the annual spectacle.

Whale Watching Sydney (from Darling Harbour, Cockle Bay Marina, tel. 02/9583-1199, www.whalewatchingsydney.net) offers a half-day "Photo Safari" (daily 2pm, $199 pp), limited to 20 passengers. This is a specialist photography trip, not a leisure cruise, guided by a professional photographer who will ensure keen amateur photographers get the best pictures they can from this trip. The boat returns after sunset, allowing for some atmospheric sunset pictures. Just in case, the photographer will also provide you with a USB drive loaded with pictures. Whale Watching Sydney also offers Sydney's fastest whale-watching trip, an "Adventure Cruise" (daily 10:30am and 2pm, adult $54, child $36, 2 hours) on the speedboat *Totally Wild*. The boat will get beyond the headlands and into the ocean within 20 minutes of departure from Darling Harbour, and due to the small size and better maneuverability of the boat, you can get closer to the animals. Do bring a waterproof jacket, as they do sometimes get very close!

Captain Cook Cruises (tel. 02/9206-1111, www.captaincook.com.au) runs "Whale Watching AM" (Aquarium Wharf, Darling Harbour, adult $90, child $57), a three-hour morning cruise with coffee and tea and live commentary throughout. They give a whale sighting guarantee, with you being able to get onto another cruise if you did not spot a whale on your trip. This is a family-friendly trip, taking it easy and slow, although the waves on the ocean can still be unpredictable.

SPECTATOR SPORTS
Stadium Tours

ANZ Stadium (Sydney Olympic Park, tel. 02/8765-2300, www.anzstadium.com.au) is a multipurpose stadium, mostly famous for the 2003 Rugby World Cup and the Olympic Games. Take the **stadium tour** (from adult $28.50, child $18.50, family $70, one hour,

whale-watching

daily except for bank holidays and special event days) and go behind the scenes, run through the players' tunnel onto the pitch, visit the changing rooms, stand on one of the Sydney Olympic medal stands, and spot your hero's autograph on the signature board.

If cricket is your passion, touring the **Sydney Cricket Ground and Allianz Stadium** (Driver Ave., Moore Park, tel. 1300/724-737, www.sydneycricketground.com.au) is a must. This **tour** (Mon.-Fri. 11am and 2pm, Sat. 11am, adult $30, child $20, family $78) takes approximately half a day, depending on the individual group's requests. It's a three-in-one tour of the Sydney Cricket Ground, the SCG Museum, and the Allianz Stadium that gives you a behind-the-scenes look at the place where plenty of sport history was written. You can see the dressing rooms, the pitch, and the members pavilion; explore the museum; experience the Allianz Stadium's field of play and players' tunnel; and learn about the sport's history.

Australian Rules Football

The season for the AFL is between March and July, and games are played across Australia. The local team is the **Sydney Swans** (www.sydneyswans.com.au). Their home ground is the **Sydney Cricket Ground** (Driver Ave., Moore Park, tel. 1300/724-737, www.sydneycricketground.com.au) and also **ANZ Stadium** (Sydney Olympic Park, tel. 02/8765-2300, www.anzstadium.com.au). For games played in Sydney, please check the website.

Cricket

Cricket is one of Australia's favorite sports. In the rest of the world, such as the cricket-mad United Kingdom, the season for this summer sport runs mid-April to September, whereas in Australia the season starts in October and ends in February or early March. During the season, all games played will be listed on the website for the **Sydney Cricket Ground** (Driver Ave., Moore Park, tel. 1300/724-737, www.sydneycricketground.com.au), together with times and prices. On game days there are food and merchandise stalls outside the stadium, making for a pleasant day out and fun for the entire family.

Soccer

The season for football (soccer) is during the Australian summer. This being the home ground of the **Sydney Football Club** (www.footballaustralia.com.au/sydneyfc), there are always plenty of games on at **Allianz**

soccer game in Sydney

Stadium (Driver Ave., Moore Park, www.scgt.nsw.gov.au). Check online for dates and tickets.

Rugby

Warathas (www.warathas.com.au) are the professional Rugby Union team of NSW and play in the Allianz Stadium. The season is during the Australian winter, and while games are played across the nation, you might be able to catch a home game.

Surfing

Held on Manly Beach in late summer (February), the nine-day **Hurley Australian Open of Surfing** (www.australianopenofsurfing.com) brings together national and international competitions from the world of surfing and skateboarding. There are also arts and live music venues set up throughout the event, making it into an all-round festival.

Yachting

Filling the harbor with sails large and small, the **Sydney to Hobart Yacht Race** (from Sydney Harbour, every Boxing Day, December 26) is a spectacle not to be missed if you are in the city. Setting off from near the Royal Botanic Gardens, scores of yachts prepare to battle against the treacherous Tasman Sea to reach Hobart, Tasmania, some 630 nautical miles away, in one of the world's most difficult races.

Horse Racing

Located relatively close to the city, **Royal Randwick Racecourse** (77-97 Alison St., Randwick, tel. 02/9663-8400, www.randwickraces.com.au) is a convenient race course to see some local and international thoroughbreds run. Races are held throughout the year, although the most famous is probably the Autumn Carnival, which is one of the richest racing carnivals in the world, held in February and March. Alternatively, there is the Spring Carnival, held in September and October each year, which is another racing—and fashion—highlight of the year's events calendar.

Dog Racing

Since the 1930s, **Wentworth Park** (Wentworth Park Rd., Glebe, tel. 02/9552-1799, www.wentworthparksport.com.au) has been the place to come to see greyhounds race. Twice a week, every Friday and Saturday night starting from 7:15pm, these sleek hounds chase the ever elusive hare around the track.

Entertainment and Events

NIGHTLIFE

Sydney is a city that can party hard, but walking around the CBD on a Saturday night, you'd be excused for thinking everybody has gone to bed early. Hot spots such as King's Cross and Darlinghurst attract the most raucous and eclectic crowds, making the most noise, but in the CBD you will have to know where to go if you want to party past midnight.

Bars

If you only go to one bar in the city, make it the **Opera Bar** (Lower Concourse Level, Sydney Opera House, tel. 02/9247-1666, www.operabar.com.au). The location is just below the opera house, on the tip of Circular Quay, opposite the bridge. Basically, the location does not get any better, and that is why this venue is *the* place for New Year's in Sydney, booked out months in advance. But NYE or not, this is simply the best place to "be" in Sydney. A little nondescript during the day, with tables and benches taking over the pavement that winds its way toward the opera house, it is the lighting and sheer atmosphere at night that makes this into a bar. The decor is the view—the furniture is comfortable enough but nothing special. This place relies fully on ambience, and that it has in spades. Sit back and soak it all up; it really is a fantastic city to watch at night over drinks. Yes, you share with the tourists, but there are also plenty of local pre-show guests. Despite that, it's relaxed and laid-back.

Near the Opera Bar is **Cruise Bar** (West Circular Quay, tel. 02/9251-1188, www.cruisebar.com.au), with another vantage point looking out across Circular Quay, the opera house, and the twinkling lights of the CBD. Relax on one of the white sofas or padded leather armchairs and enjoy the setting. On the weekend there's a DJ livening things up a little, but generally this is a relatively low-key place to have a drink or two off the cocktail list before moving onto dinner, a show, or a club. It is open in the daytime, but at night the lights of the city make it really special.

Just opposite Circular Quay in The Rocks is **Bar 100** (100 George St., The Rocks, tel. 02/8070-9311, www.bar100.com.au). Bar 100, strictly speaking, is a cocktail bar in a stunning historic building (the Mariners' Church, established in 1856), but in reality it is several venues in one, ranging from the heritage-look setting to a modern rooftop bar to a dining room and an old-fashioned lounge. Drifting from venue to venue is a great way to spend a night on The Rocks. You can get a wide selection of drinks plus bar snacks and other food (pizza $22, kangaroo burger $20).

Around the corner from Bar 100 is **Eric's Bar—Searching for Scarlett** (34 Harrington St., The Rocks, tel. 02/8220-9999, www.scarlettrestaurant.com.au). A lovely little bar on the ground floor of the Harbour Rocks Hotel, it is reportedly named after Eric, a merchant sailor in the late 1800s who was in love with Scarlett, a madam who ran the brothel next door. It's a romantic setting, full of character, incorporating modern furniture into the historic setting, with quirky decor, such as the lovely map mural of old Sydney Cove. The bar offers a great choice of grapes as well as bar snacks to share, such as edamame or potato wedges ($7 per plate).

On the way into the CBD from The Rocks is **Grain** (Four Seasons Hotel, 199 George St., CBD, tel. 02/9250-3100, www.fourseasons.com/Sydney), a small, comfortable bar on the ground floor of the Four Seasons Hotel that is also accessible from the outside. The Grain moniker refers not just to the drinks but also to the smooth wood decor. Dotted with beautiful pieces of art, this is a quiet place to have a beverage before contemplating the night out.

The ArtHouse Hotel (275 Pitt St., CBD, tel. 02/9284-1200, www.thearthousehotel.com.au) lies in the heart of the CBD. Dating back to 1836, this heritage-listed building right in the heart of the city center originally was Sydney's School of Arts and later served as a theater, a library, and even a chapel before reinventing itself as a bar—or bars, as there are three venues in one. True to its name, the bar doubles as a gallery, and the ArtHouse hosts a few dozen exhibitions every year, plus it regularly stages creative arts events such as life drawing, burlesque and cabaret variety nights, and photography workshops. It is an impressive venue in a great location and a place to hunker down and stay awhile.

The elegant decor of **Black Bar** (Harbourside Entrance, The Star, Pirrama Rd., Pyrmont, tel. 02/9777-9000, www.star.com.au), in the entertainment complex of The Star just off Darling Harbour, evokes the 1920s with stylish surroundings and bartenders wearing crisp white shirts and suspenders. The twirling and whirling young men are reviving pre-prohibition cocktails and some long forgotten drinks. Look out for the hand-chiseled, diamond-shaped ice cubes and the Brunch Cocktail, the signature orange drink on everybody's lips.

While Kings Cross can be a little seedy, **Hugo's Lounge** (33 Bayswater Rd., Kings Cross, tel. 02/9357-4411, www.hugos.com.au) is chic personified. All the cool people of Sydney seem to mingle here sipping their champagne or trying out new cocktails, adding a touch of sparkle to the black stone walls, black couches, black floors, and cream ottomans. It's very stylish, very elegant, and from the rooftop you have great views out and over the seedier life below.

Down the road from Kings Cross in Woolloomooloo is the **Water Bar** (6 Cowper Wharf Rd., Woolloomooloo, tel. 02/9331-9000, www.waterbaratblue.com). Continuously winning awards and having been named "Bar of the Year" by numerous magazines—and even notching up a "Top Ten Bars in the World" accolade from *Condé Nast Traveler*—the Water Bar is huge and swanky, combining industrial warehouse heritage with sparkling Swarovski crystal water-drop curtains. Inside the BLUE Sydney Hotel on Woolloomooloo Wharf, you are surrounded by top-notch restaurants, such as Otto Ristorante, so a pre- or après-dinner drink is certainly called for.

If you are in Bondi, look no further than the **Neighbourhood** (143 Curlweis St., Bondi, tel. 02/9365-2872, http://neighbourhoodbondi.com.au). Bare brick walls, retro lighting, and shabby-chic leather armchairs add to the general laid-back Bondi beach atmosphere. The broadcasting studio of the since-departed Bondi 88.0 FM radio station in the bar has been taken over by new Bondi Radio, promising 24-hour entertainment and broadcasting from right there. The bar prides itself on innovative and seasonal drinks, always offering something out of the ordinary.

Dance Clubs

If you want to go clubbing in Sydney, it's easy to catch up with a few clubs right in the CBD and nearby neighborhoods. **Chinese Laundry** (111 Sussex St., CBD, tel. 02/8295-9999, http://chineselaundryclub.com.au, cover $25, varies), colloquially known simply as the "Laundry," is one of Sydney's biggest and most popular dance clubs. The professional sound system in the "Cave," another chill-out room in the club, has attracted heavyweight internationals such as James Holden, Gui Boratto, and Sasha, with local and visiting DJs hosting nights every weekend, and the outdoor dance floor is the place for summer clubbing.

Ivy (1/330 George St., CBD, tel. 02/9254-8100, http://merivale.com.au/ivy, cover Saturday nights minimum $20) is a truly mammoth complex, boasting 13 venues, right in the center of the city. Venues include restaurants, secluded lounges, the exclusive but not members-only rooftop Pool Club, and bars. Most importantly, there is **Pacha,** the huge dance venue with sky-high ceilings and a packed floor hosting DJs and pool parties. It was voted "Dance Club of the Year" in 2013. Then there is the Changeroom, with actual lockers and changing rooms. It reportedly is the city's most popular hetero pseudo sex-club with a dance floor, so be careful of which floor you step out of the elevator.

Less overwhelming than Ivy is **The Spice Cellar** (58 Elizabeth St., CBD, tel. 02/9223-5585, http://thespicecellar.com.au, $10 to $20 for events). Sydney DJ Murat Killic teamed up with club promoters Warren Faulkner and Rebecca Alder to create a much-needed halfway point between bar-hopping and clubbing for the city's nightlife enthusiasts. There is a cocktail lounge for late afternoon drinks, a tapas bar for sustenance, and on weekends the Spice Cellar hosts local and visiting DJs and stays open until 10am.

Just slightly out of the CBD toward Ultimo is **Abercrombie** (corner Broadway St. and Abercrombie St., Broadway, tel. 02/9280-2178, free). This is a hotel (a.k.a. pub) turned techno den, with the Strange Fruit parties on Saturday nights bringing in the crowds, probably mostly owing to the free entry. Featuring plenty of regular DJs, this place is popular with students due to its proximity to TAFE (Training and Further Education) Ultimo College.

In the bustling alternative nightlife scene that is Darlinghurst's Oxford Street, **The Exchange Hotel** (44 Oxford St., Darlinghurst, tel. 02/9331-2956, http://exchangesydney.com.au, cover varies) features several venues, such as the **Q Bar,** the dance hot spot with plenty of funk and house; **Spectrum,** hosting mostly live music in an intimate 250-capacity venue; subterranean **Phoenix,** hosting a slightly older crowd with an eclectic mix of dance music; and **34B,** the burlesque venue with regular shows on the roster.

GLBT

Darlinghurst's Oxford Street has a heavy dose of gay and lesbian bars, clubs, shops, and general scene. Start the night at **The Midnight Shift** (85 Oxford St., Darlinghurst, tel. 02/9358-3848, daily 2pm-late, Fri.-Sat. even later), Sydney's oldest gay venue, which is packed with full shows, featuring entertainment every night.

Arq (16 Flinders St., Darlinghurst, tel. 02/9380-8700, Thurs.-Sun. 9pm to early morning) is one of Sydney's largest clubs, with an enormous dance floor, light and laser shows, and a bustling mezzanine floor overlooking the dancers. Four nights a week entertainment features Drags to Riches dance competitions, Drag'n'Fly shows, go-go boy strippers, dancers in cat outfits, and so much more.

A (formerly) traditional pub, **The Oxford Hotel** (134 Oxford St., Darlinghurst, tel. 02/8324-5200, daily 10am-4am) is a mix of gay and straight, open-minded and eclectic. Downstairs in the Underground Bar with its brick arches, you can find music, lasers, inner sprung dance floor, pinball machines, and plenty of unconventional people.

Live Music

There are plenty of live music venues throughout the city, although you might have to jump into a taxi to get to some of them. Right in the CBD is **The Basement** (29 Reiby Place, Circular Quay, CBD, tel. 02/9251-2797, www.thebasement.com.au). This little basement (literally) is primarily a jazz venue with the likes of Dizzy Gillespie having played here in its 40-year history. There is a steady list of local and international contemporary musicians and jazz bands playing here nearly daily, with special events held on certain occasions. It's a great venue in a bustling location.

The historic **Marble Bar** (Level B1, 488 George St., CBD, Hilton Sydney, tel. 02/9266-2000, http://marblebarsydney.com.au) is also conveniently located in the city's center. It would be worth seeing, even if you weren't heading there for live music. Built in 1893, this high-ceilinged Victorian bar was not originally raised in the place it is now but was painstakingly dismantled and re-erected in the current site. With marble columns, fireplaces, and over-the-top but well-suited past-age decor, this place is a piece of history and hosts live music every Wednesday to Saturday evening, with bands ranging from R&B and soul to '80s mixes, from jazzy to cover versions of rock classics.

In bustling Kings Cross and Darlinghurst you can find more venues, such as **FBi Social** (Kings Cross Hotel, 244-248 William St., Kings Cross, tel. 02/9331-9900, www.kingscrosshotel.com.au), which lines up some of the best local bands and DJs alongside a carefully selected lineup of international acts. During the week you'll find a variety of shows to supplement the music on the weekends, such as open mic nights, comedy fixtures, and even some poetry.

The World Bar (24 Bayswater Rd., Kings Cross, tel. 02/9357-7700, www.theworldbar.com) can be found in the unlikely location of a three-story Victorian terrace house. This venue is an odd combination of historic club lounge (complete with leather settees, chandeliers, old dials, and knickknacks), tea room, and trendy bar. This strangely likable setup is a mix of bar, club, and live music venue, and offers something different at every turn.

The **Oxford Art Factory** (38-46 Oxford St., Darlinghurst, tel. 02/9332-3711, www.oxfordartfactory.com) offers visual art, performance art, and live music. The concept is based on Andy Warhol's New York Factory, providing an edgy venue and myriad performance spaces. Most of the live music performances are local bands that play for free.

A little farther out toward the city's southwest is the **Lazybones Lounge** (Level 2, 294 Marrickville Rd., Marrickville, tel. 04/8875-9548, http://lazyboneslounge.com.au), but it is well worth the trip. Set up like someone's living room complete with bookshelves, old couches, chandeliers, and knickknacks, this venue is a music lounge with live music seven nights a week, ranging from jazz to DJs on Saturday nights. Local beers and ciders are on tap. The atmosphere is relaxed, with comfort food coming from the kitchen, including South African street food such as the famed Bunny Chow, a type of curry served in hollowed-out bread. Sit back, relax, enjoy the music.

Shows

Sydney has some great dinner shows, some burlesque, some magic, all in great venues and fun. Try the **Crystal Boudoir** (GPO, 1 Martin Place, CBD, tel. 02/9229-7799, www.gposydney.com, Sat. 8:30pm-2am, $85 for a two-course meal). Right in the heart of the city, in the gorgeous old General Post Office building, this is a glamorous bar, restaurant, and show venue. In the dimly lit yet sparkling room there are choreographed dancers performing a variety of acts, from flamenco to burlesque to contortions. It has a distinctive Parisian 1920s nightclub atmosphere in historical surroundings.

El' Circo (41 Oxford St., Darlinghurst, tel. 02/8915-1899, http://slide.com.au, selected Fri. and Sat. nights 7pm, $109 pp) is hidden away from hopping Oxford Street. You come in through a door you'd nearly walk past and enter a cave of fun. Enjoy a nine-course degustation menu combined with nine circus acts. Created by French-born Marc Kuzma, El' Circo features circus acts influenced with the mysterious charm and flavor of Parisian or Berlin cabaret.

Or why not hop on a boat? Sydney is all about the harbor, after all. Set sail with **Sydney Showboats** (32 The Promenade, King Street Wharf 5, Darling Harbour, tel. 02/8296-7200, www.sydneyshowboats.com.au, from $120 pp) on an old-fashioned showboat and sail past the Sydney Harbour Bridge, Sydney Opera House, and the various islands while enjoying a three-course dinner on board. Then watch the one-hour show full of cancan dancing, sequins, feathers, and fishnet stockings—lively and fun.

THE ARTS

There is a thriving arts scene in Sydney. Be it visual art, performance art, music, or dance, Sydney offers many venues and events, but dates change and it is best to check what's on when you know your dates of travel. Certain organizations always showcase something interesting, however. This is a selection of permanent venues.

The Archibald Prize is Australia's most prestigious and controversial art award and has been going strong since 1921. It is awarded to the best portrait painting. Each year the trustees of the Art Gallery of NSW judge the Archibald and Wynne Prizes (awarded to best Australian landscape painting or figure sculpture) and invite an artist to judge the Sulman Prize (awarded to best subject painting, genre painting, or mural project in oil, acrylic, watercolor, or mixed media). The **Archibald Prize** (Art Gallery of NSW, The Domain) is held usually in fall or winter, but dates vary. All contenders for the prizes are shown and you're allowed to vote for your favorite portrait in the People's Choice award.

Bangarra (Pier 4, 15 Hickson Rd., Walsh Bay, tel. 02/9251-5333, www.bangarra.com.au) is Australia's leading Aboriginal performing arts company, weaving traditional and modern cultures seamlessly into its award-winning contemporary dance theater productions. Stunning, modern, challenging, and thought-provoking, the performances and productions are a new way of telling the indigenous stories. There are always several productions ongoing throughout the year, at different venues, such as the Sydney Opera House, and the company travels throughout Australia, so please check the calendar for dates.

The **Belvoir** (18 & 25 Belvoir St., Surry Hills, tel. 02/9699-3444, http://Belvoir.com.au), one of Australia's most pioneering and celebrated theater companies, has continuously made landmark productions available to the public and has over the years earned a myriad of prize nominations, and subsequent wins. Some have since been staged in New York, such as the 2013 production of *Peter Pan*. Both the Upstairs and Downstairs stages at the Belvoir have fostered the talents of prominent Australian artists, such as actors Geoffrey Rush and Cate Blanchett.

In the brick-and-iron buildings of the old Eveleigh Railyards, built between 1880 and 1889, **Carriageworks** (245 Wilson St., Eveleigh, tel. 02/8571-9099, http://carriageworks.com.au) hosts a diverse lineup of experimental music, theater, film, and fine art exhibitions. The largest multi-art venue in the country, it is home to contemporary arts organizations.

Sydney Theatre Company (The Wharf, Pier 4, Hickson Rd., Walsh Bay, tel. 02/9250-1700, www.sydneytheatre.com.au) is the premier theater company in Australia, and a major force in Australian drama since its establishment in 1978. The company presents an annual 12- to 13-play program at its home base, The Wharf; at the nearby new Sydney Theatre (22 Hickson Rd., Walsh Bay, tel.02/9250-1999), which Sydney Theatre Company also manages; and as the resident theater company of the Sydney Opera House.

The **Sydney Conservatorium of Music** (corner Bridge St. and Macquarie St., tel. 02/9351-1438, http://music.sydney.edu.au, Mon.-Sat. 8am-6pm, free) is open to visitors to inspect the eclectic architecture of its buildings, made up of a colonial main building, stables, and modern additions, making for a seemingly fortified structure reminiscent of a European castle. Bear in mind that it is a working school and performance venue, so access to some areas is not permitted. Regular concerts by students and visiting artists are held in the venue. For a schedule of events check the website.

FESTIVALS AND EVENTS

Australians love nothing better than a good party, and any excuse will do. The main annual events are listed here. For a detailed and up-to-date calendar of what's on when you are in the city, check www.visitnsw.com/events.

January

- **Australia Day** (www.australiaday.com.au): On January 26, Australians celebrate the spirit of Australia Day, which commemorates the arrival of the First Fleet, always making it into a long weekend filled with parades, music, events, barbecues, and lots of fun all across the city and the entire country.

- **Sydney Festival** (www.sydneyfestival.org.au): The city erupts into a frenzy of performing arts with over a fortnight of concerts, plays, circuses, and dance. There are some 300 performances in 100 events executed by more than 1,000 artists at various venues. The festival usually runs between January 8 or 9 until the 26th, depending on the days of the week.

February

- **Chinese New Year** (www.sydneychinesenewyear.com.au): Celebrate the Lunar New Year in late January or February, together with Sydney's large Chinese population. Numerous events, markets, and parades are held in Chinatown and throughout the city.

- **Sydney Gay & Lesbian Mardi Gras** (www.mardigras.org.au): Ongoing throughout the month, this is undoubtedly the biggest and most colorful parade and party in town. It attracts more than 20,000 visitors each year. Festivities are held on Oxford Street and at various venues.

March

- **Sydney Harbour Regatta** (www.shrmhyc.com.au): Watch beautiful boats in a beautiful setting. More than 300 yachts and

Welcoming the New Year

There is no doubt that Sydney is naturally one of the most stunning cities on this Earth, but when it wants to, it can even improve on its natural beauty. Being one of the first cities to welcome a New Year, its fireworks spectacular has been watched by millions around the world, usually on television. But if you are in Australia, a visit to Sydney at New Year is an absolute must. There simply is no better celebration to watch live.

One of the first things to remember is that New Year down under falls in the middle of the summer holidays, so there is no need to wrap up warm—just put on your summery glad rags. Then, whatever you are planning to do, book early—organized venues and events places are limited and very sought-after.

The main focus of the celebrations is the **Sydney Harbour Bridge,** or the "old coat hanger," as it is affectionately known. A view of the opera house and the bridge are preferable, but fireworks are let off throughout the harbor, and a star-spangled flotilla of boats parades through the length of the harbor between the **two main fireworks events.** Yes, there are two occasions to see the magic happening in the sky: Traditionally Sydney sends off the first volley of fireworks at 9pm for the younger generation, and then the proper full works go off at midnight. The 9pm version is a smaller teaser-version of the fireworks to follow later on, but it's designed for the children, who can then be safely sent off to bed.

The **best place** to enjoy the night is on a **boat in the harbor,** and it is amazing how by midnight the water seems to have pretty much disappeared beneath the sea of boats. All types and sizes are puttering around the waterways, full of revelers and merry-makers. Many are private vessels, but plenty are ferries and cruise ships on which tickets for the night can be secured. Tickets usually include dinner, dancing, and a glass of bubbly at midnight, and prices range from 200 to several hundred dollars. Try the following companies: **All Occasion Cruises** (www.aocruises.com.au), **Sydney Harbour Cruises** (www.sydneyharbourcruises.com.au), **Stars Cruising Nightclub** (www.starscruisingnightclub.com.au), **Bass & Flinders Cruises** (www.newyearsevecruise.com.au), **Vagabond Cruises** (www.vagabond.com.au).

The **cheapest way** to enjoy the night is by **coming early,** and I mean early: Surprisingly, many camp overnight, and by 10am the really good spots are already taken, especially those by the opera house, at Mrs Macquarie's Chair in the Royal Botanic Gardens, or on any of the north shore beaches overlooking the bridge. This obviously takes planning and dedication, especially as numbers admitted and items taken are limited and scrutinized by security, ensuring that people don't get too squashed.

2,500 crew compete inshore and offshore, over two days of racing, on eight course areas and over 24 divisions. It's usually held the second weekend of the month.

- **Royal Easter Show** (www.eastershow.com.au): Since 1823 this nearly two-week-long event has celebrated Australia's best produce by showcasing animals, agricultural produce, free entertainment, and lots of fun. It's held at Sydney Olympic Park at the end of the month, running into April.

- **Opera on the Harbour** (http://opera-onsydneyharbour.com.au): Once a year for a stretch of around six weeks, Sydney Opera moves to Farm Cove and performs under the stars in the most magical setting, overlooking the Sydney Opera House and Sydney Harbour Bridge with the Domain behind you.

April

- **Biennale of Sydney** (www.biennaleofsydney.com.au): Australia's largest contemporary visual arts event, presenting artist talks, performances, forums, exhibitions, and tours at various venues. It's held every two years, usually from the end of March until June.

New Year's Eve fireworks in Sydney Harbour

If you can afford a **splurge,** then being squashed need not be an issue and you can enjoy dinner and drinks in one of the many **hotels and bars** overlooking the harbor. But you will need to book early and be prepared to part with several hundred dollars per person for the privilege. Some of the best and priciest hot spots for the night are the **Shangri La** (www.shangri-la.com), with its suites overlooking the harbor and restaurants putting on special menus; the bar at the top of the Sydney Tower, **360 Bar & Dining** (www.trippaswhitegroup.com.au); or indeed the **Opera Bar** (www.operabar.com.au) below the opera house, where an entrance fee of some $300 is charged, excluding drinks.

Either way, it is a night not to be missed, and whatever your budget, Sydney does its best not to disappoint, and you will certainly welcome the New Year in a spectacular fashion. Check out www.sydneynewyearseve.com for planning tips and a program of events.

- **Mercedes-Benz Fashion Week Australia** (www.mbfashionweek.com.au): Usually held in mid-April for a week, this fashion extravaganza showcases Australia's emerging and established talent.

- **ANZAC Day:** On April 25, Australia remembers those who gave their lives in service to the country. Parades, memorial services, and celebrations are held throughout the city and country.

May

- **Vivid Sydney** (www.vividsydney.com): See the opera house lit up in psychedelic colors during this unique annual event of light, music, and ideas. Public exhibitions of outdoor light sculptures and installations, creative forums, concerts, and performances are held over a fortnight, usually at the end of the month into June.

June

- **Sydney Film Festival** (www.sff.org.au): Since 1954 (making it one of the world's longest running film festivals), this 12-day event held in mid-June has celebrated the best in Australian and international film, shorts, and documentaries.

July

- **Splendour in the Grass** (http://splendourinthegrass.com): One of Australia's biggest outdoor music festivals, this event stretches over three days with always great lineups. It's held at Byron Bay, just south of the city, at the end of the month.

August

- **City to Surf** (www.city2surf.com.au): In mid-August is Sydney's favorite sporting event and the world's largest run, with around 85,000 registered participants each year. The 14-kilometer course takes runners from Hyde Park to Bondi Beach.

- **Sydney Spring Racing Carnival** (www.australianturfclub.com.au): Held at Royal Randwick and Rosehill Gardens, this important day in horse racing is also a great excuse to get that hat out. Dates vary.

September

- **Festival of the Winds** (www.waverley.nsw.gov.au): Is there anything more beautiful to see in a beach setting and on a blue sky than colorful kites? The festival is held at Bondi Beach, along with markets, music, and lots of fun, usually from mid-September until early October.

October

- **Opera in the Vineyards** (www.operainthevineyards.com.au): Since 1995, this annual celebration of food, wine, and opera has been held in the beautiful Hunter Valley.

November

- **Sculpture by the Sea** (www.sculpturebythesea.com): Stretching along one of Australia's most scenic walks from Bondi Beach to Tamarama Beach, stunning sculptures are placed to enhance the already stunning views. It's usually held from late October to mid-November.

December

- **Carols in the Domain** (www.carolsinthedomain.com): Get into the Christmas mood even though the sun is shining by attending this traditional carol singing event in the Domain, usually held on December 21 or 22.

- **Rolex Sydney to Hobart Yacht Race** (www.rolexsydneyhobart.com): Held since 1945, this is the most iconic of yacht races down under. Participants from maxi yachts to weekend racers take part in this event, which starts from Nielsen Park in Sydney Harbour and takes the international fleet 628 nautical miles to the finish line in the Derwent River, Hobart. The race starts in Sydney on Boxing Day, December 26, and usually takes four days, but arrivals vary.

- **New Year's Eve** (www.sydneynewyearseve.com, www.new-years-eve-in-sydney.com): Sydney is the place to be at New Year's. On December 31, countless venues across the city hold celebrations, and fireworks can be seen.

Shopping

SHOPPING DISTRICTS AND SHOPPING CENTERS

Paddington is the hub of chic and contemporary Australian fashion and then some. Saunter along Oxford Street and find trendy fashion boutiques, quirky accessory shops, and the walk of fashion, a stretch of sidewalk dotted with plaque celebrating Australia's fashion-influencers, where you can test your Australian fashion knowledge. To see what shops are where, pick up an *Urban Walkabouts* booklet in any visitors center, or download the map at www.urbanwalkabout.com/paddington.

The **Queen Victoria Building (QVB)** (455 George St., CBD, tel. 02/9265-6800, www.qvb.com.au, lower ground and ground floors open Mon.-Sat. 9am-6pm, Sun. 11am-5pm; Level 1 and Level 2 open Mon.-Sat. 10am-6pm, Sun. 11am-5pm) is possibly the prettiest and grandest shopping mall in the world. First opened in 1898, the building replaced the old Sydney Markets and housed a hotel, a concert hall, numerous shops, warehouses, and markets in the basement. The Romanesque building, which was remodeled in the 1930s and then again restored in the mid-1980s, now houses numerous shops, cafés, and restaurants. Very generally speaking, it gets more expensive the higher up you go, with many designer stores such as Ralph Lauren on the upper levels and high street shops, services, and food courts in the basement. However, it's not just the shopping you come here for but the building itself: At Christmas the mid-entrance is literally filled with a gigantic Christmas tree, the toilets are well worth a visit for their heritage beauty, and even the staircases are pretty.

Built in the 1880s, the Victorian building housing the **Strand Arcade** (412-414 George St., CBD, tel. 02/9232-4199, www.strandarcade.com.au, Mon., Tues., Wed., Fri. 9am-5:30pm, Thurs. 9am-8pm, Sat. 9am-4pm, Sun. 11am-4pm) was one of the first in Sydney designed to take into account the harsh Australian climate. The roof was to be made of glass, specially tinted to reduce glare, and the access gallery of the top floor was projected to shade the lower levels. This is a lovely old shopping arcade in the vein of the Burlington Arcade in London, and then as now it is a refuge from the bustling George and Pitt Street shops, a collection of classy, high-quality select individual shops that reflect a bygone era. Stop for a hot chocolate and watch people saunter past. No rushing here—take your time and spend lots of time window shopping and browsing. It's part of the fun.

Westfield Sydney (188 Pitt St., CBD, tel. 02/8236-9200, www.westfield.com.au/sydney, Mon.-Sat. 9:30am-7pm, Sun. 10am-6pm) is a fantastic inner-city mall that offers anything and everything from luxury designer goods to home decor and gifts. Think Gucci and Prada, and think Zara and Gap—it's all under one roof. Spread over six shopping levels, it also allows access to Sydney Tower Eye and the 360 Bar & Dining restaurant and offers valet parking and a concierge desk, should you need help deciding.

CLOTHING AND ACCESSORIES

Nearly every big city has a **Burberry** (343 George St., CBD, tel. 02/8296-8588, http://au.burberry.com, daily 10am-6pm), Sydney being no exception. What makes this one special is the building. A former bank building, it is huge, with high ceilings and marble columns throughout. The sheer glamour of the surroundings making shopping here either better or quite unnecessary—just go for a look around.

When in Australia you'll find yourself needing a hat to protect you against the fierce

Stylish Sydney

Sydney is Australia's fashion capital and is flash, modern, rich, and stylish. The country's best designers have their seats here, and shopping has evolved to an art form. Here's where to stay, eat, shop, and, of course, be seen.

HOTELS

QT Hotel is part film set, part art gallery, part Las Vegas showgirls, with a dash of luxury bordello thrown in the mix. The hotel has taken over an old theater and has kept the grandeur, illusion, and eccentricity of that world. See and be seen.

Smaller but just as trendy, **Establishment Hotel** offers a fashionable stay in a former warehouse. Exposed brick balances the understated elegance; cushions offer a splash of color against sophisticated minimalist hues; and the heritage-meets-fashion theme is carried throughout.

SHOPS

Head for the **Queen Victoria Building (QVB)** to experience what is probably the chicest mall there is: This late-1800s structure is magnificent in its own right, with stunning architecture and intricate decor details. The great old building has been filled with myriad shops that have been selected to enhance the experience. Down below, you'll find the quite literal bargain basement. The higher up you go, the pricier and classier the shops, selling designer clothing, exquisite modern as well as antique jewelry, and accessories.

The Victorian **Strand Arcade** is great for browsing shops in the old-world style, complete with old-world service. Shops offer anything from cufflinks to hand-made shoes, from superb leather wares to beautiful straw hats.

To sample some of Australia's finest fashion, head straight for **Paddington.** Follow the fashion walk, with stars given to the local design talent. Snoop around the quirky individual boutiques for the latest trends and scoop up some unique accessories and decor items before relaxing in one of the many little cafés.

FOOD AND DRINK

Take pre- or après-dinner drinks at the **Opera Bar,** with its stunning views and eclectic clientele.

---

sun. **Hatworld** (81 George St., The Rocks, tel. 02/9252-3525, daily 9:30am-7:30pm) not only sells the iconic Outback Akura hats, worn by the truly rugged types, but also great straw hats, panamas, fedoras, and all sorts of head coverings, in a good range of sizes. Here you can go for quality rather than a last-minute purchase at the airport.

If you are looking for a good quality bag, suitcase, or any type of leather accessory, **Hunt Leather** (412 George St., CBD, tel. 02/9233-8702, www.huntleather.com.au, Mon.-Wed. 9am-6pm, Thurs. 9am-8pm, Sat. 9am-5pm, Sun. 11am-5pm) is the shop to look for it. Elegant, understated, timeless, yet modern, the items are lovely and you won't find them dangling from every other arm.

Originally started in Melbourne, **Shag** (34 Oxford St., Paddington, tel. 02/9357-2475, daily around noon-6pm) is a great vintage store stocking clothing (including pretty petticoat dresses and men's tuxedos), costume jewelry, bags and accessories from the 1920s to the 1970s, leather jackets, and tweeds, and you might even find the odd luxury designer treasure. It takes time to look through all the offerings, but the staff is knowledgable and can find things for you, even if you don't know what you want.

The Intersection (corner Oxford St. and Glenmore Rd., Paddington, tel. 02/4888-2359, www.theintersectionpaddington.com.au) is a fashion shopping destination developed with the clear vision to create a unique

shopping in the Queen Victoria Building

Anything goes, from long dresses prior to an opera event to touristy sneakers and backpacks, but you still can't beat the style and location.

Then move along to **Quay,** one of Sydney's best restaurants, where you might know the ingredients on the menu, but you'll be surprised by what the celebrity chef does with them. The inside is just as fashionable as the views across to the opera house, and you'll probably spot a celebrity or two as well.

FASHION

The annual **Mercedes-Benz Fashion Week Australia,** usually held around April, lures international fashion buyers, media, and celebrities to the city, which in turn dresses the part with many store windows designed to showcase participating designers.

retail environment focused exclusively around Australian designers. Numerous individual boutiques showcase the latest designers, high fashion but wearable and varied. Brands include Willow, Scanlan & Theodore, Jac + Jack, Ginger/Smart, and Ksubi. Hours vary per boutique, but most are open between 10am and 5:30pm.

Vanishing Elephant (Shop 3022, Westfield Bondi Junction, Bondi Junction, tel. 02/9389-4138, Mon.-Fri. 9:30am-6pm, Thurs. 9:30am-9pm, Sun. 10am-6pm) is a men's clothing store where you can get the perfect white shirt or checked shirt, cords, khakis, and more—stylish and modern yet classic outfits for work and leisure, designed by men for men.

GIFTS

With 95 percent of the world's opals being mined in Australia, it seems to be an obvious souvenir and gift, but there are so many different varieties and range in quality that expert advice is needed. **Australian Opal Cutters** (3/295-301 Pitt St., CBD, tel. 02/9261-2442, www.australianopalcutters.com, Mon.-Fri. 9am-6pm, Sat. 9am-5pm, Sun. 10am-5pm) has one of the largest selections of opals in Australia and knowledgable staff who can advise you.

Gannon House Gallery (45 Argyle St., The Rocks, tel. 02/9251-4474, www.gannonhousegallery.com, daily 10am-6pm) offers a great selection of Aboriginal and contemporary Australian art pieces for sale, ranging from lantern domes painted in the naive style that depict the Sydney cityscape to huge dotted paintings. While the vast Aboriginal paintings often cost a small fortune, smaller pieces are also typically Australian, and they make great gifts or souvenirs.

The museum shop **MCA** (Museum of Contemporary Art, 140 George St., The Rocks, tel. 02/9245-2458, Thurs. 10am-9pm, Fri.-Wed. 10am-5pm) is the place to find gifts that are a little out of the ordinary, including handcrafted jewelry, bags, unique home wares, limited edition artists' books (often signed), stationery, coffee-table books, and prints.

If you are looking for something quirky, **OPUS** (344 Oxford St., Paddington, tel. 02/9360-4803, Mon.-Sat. 10am-6pm, Sun. 11am-5pm) is your store, with lovely journals, select travel guides, assorted Sydney walks on playing cards, small home decor items, kitchen wares, gadgets and novelty items for the office, and more. It is impossible to leave without a little something.

Victoria's Basement (Queen Victoria Building, George St., tel. 02/9261-2674, Mon.-Sat. 9am-6pm, Sun. 11am-5pm) is a cheap, fun place to rummage for home items and great, lightweight souvenirs such as linen tea towels imprinted with Australian themes or Sydney cityscapes. It's definitely worth a look while you're in the QVB.

ANTIQUES AND CURIOS

Sydney Antique Centre (531 S. Dowling St., Surry Hills, tel. 02/9361-3244, www.sydantcent.com.au, daily 10am-6pm) is one of Australia's largest and oldest antiques centers, complete with café. With Australia being home to immigrants from all across the globe, the finds here can range from Art Deco French glass to Japanese netsuke, from Australiana to German china. With collectibles, jewelry, and even vintage clothing, this is a haven for treasure hunters.

Located in the basement of the Metcalf Arcade in The Rocks, **Bottom of the Harbour** (Metcalfe Arcade, 80 George St., The Rocks, tel. 02/9427-8107, Tues., Wed., Sat., and Sun. 9:30am-5:30pm, Mon., Thurs., and Fri. 9:30am-3:30pm) specializes in maritime antiques, curios, and trinkets. You can find anything from ship's steering wheels to glass floating devices and old coins. It's fun to rummage through, and maybe you'll find a pirate's treasure.

BOOKS

Ariel Booksellers (103 George St., The Rocks, tel. 02/9241-5622, www.arielbooks.com.au, daily 9am-late) is a lovely little bookshop specializing in coffee-table books covering architecture, art, design, and photography. It also sells the latest novels and a great assortment of kids' books. Together with its sister shop in Paddington (42 Oxford St., tel. 02/9332-4581, daily 9am-late), this is an independent venture and staffed by knowledgable and interested employees.

Probably Australia's best-loved book store, **Dymocks** (The Dymocks Building, 428 George St., CBD, tel. 02/9235-0155, Mon.-Fri. 9am-7pm, Thurs. till 9pm, Sat. 9:30am-5pm, Sun. 10am-5pm) is the Dymocks flagship store, going back to 1879 when young William Dymock commenced business as a bookseller in nearby Market Street. In 1922, the Dymock family started to build the historic, Art Deco landmark Dymocks building, completed in 1930. The store is very pretty, with an open mezzanine floor and wooden banisters keeping readers from toppling down. Dymocks has a great selection of books, some special offers, an assortment of great gifts, and a coffee shop in the back.

What goes together better than coffee and books? The cozy little **Gertrude & Alice Café Bookstore** (46 Hall St., Bondi Beach, tel. 02/9130-5155, weekdays 7:30am-11pm, weekends 7:30am-noon), lined with vintage books, was named after Gertrude Stein and Alice B. Toklas, and is always busy with people taking their time over their steaming cup of chai and browsing the shelves. There are some truly beautiful old editions of Australian kids' stories and many books paying homage to the owners' love of the 1920s and 1930s Paris literary circles.

Elizabeth's Books (343 Pitt St., CBD, tel. 02/9267-2533, www.elizabethsbookshop.com.au) sells both new and used books. An independent small bookstore, it offers little quirks the giant stores simply don't, such as a shelf full of books wrapped in brown paper, with merely two clues on the front as to what the story is about: "marooned on island" and "thriller," says one; "Australia" and "romance" says another. A great way to be a little more adventurous and discover new authors.

The Singaporean bookstore giant **Kinokuniya** (Level 2, The Galleries, 500 George St., CBD, tel. 02/9262-7996) is not quite as gigantic here in Sydney as elsewhere in the world, but it still has a fantastic selection of all current and classic books, with a nice travel corner. There's a good Asian selection, too, covering books about Asia, by Asian authors, and various Asian-language titles.

Accommodations

Sydney is a large, cosmopolitan city, and you can find a vast variety of accommodation options here. But it is expensive. As a general guideline, although there are youth hostels and budget options, you should allow around $200 per night for a basic room. Anything below that is a bonus. That said, if you book well in advance and take advantage of special offers, you should hopefully be able to secure something central and budget-friendly. The local transport system is fantastic, with trains easily accessed and taking you all across the city for a good price, but while you might save some money by staying a little farther out of town, finding accommodations near the center and paying a little extra is often worth it for the time and effort saved. Being able to walk back to your hotel for an afternoon rest is often the traveler's savior when sight-seeing. Room prices quoted are usually for the most basic double room, low-season, without breakfast unless mentioned.

THE ROCKS AND CIRCULAR QUAY
Under $150

Located at the south end of The Rocks toward the CBD, **The Menzies** (14 Carrington St., tel. 02/9299-1000, www.sydneymenzieshotel.com.au, from $149) offers basic but clean and comfortable standard rooms in single, double, and triple configuration. They are spacious enough to accommodate a family with up to two kids, while the superior rooms and suites offer separate living areas and more space. There is a breakfast restaurant, and three bars offer bar snacks, coffees, and wines. The hotel is a 1960s build, once a sought-after address that now has lost some of its initial accolade of being the first international hotel built after World War II. Despite its now quite stark exterior, it is a good value place to stay.

Napoleon on Kent (219 Kent St., tel. 02/9299-5588, http://napoleononkent.etourism.com.au, studio from $104) has very basic apartments in a modern-build block right underneath a thundering flyover along a relatively busy road, but the facilities are all there, and the rooms are modern and comfortable, with private baths and coffee-making facilities. The larger apartments have separate dining areas and kitchenettes. Not necessarily somewhere to linger, but if you're out all day and want somewhere cheap (for Sydney) to sleep, you could do a lot worse.

★ **Sydney Harbour YHA** (110 Cumberland St., tel. 02/8272-0900, www.yha.com.au, dorm beds from $39 pp per night, double rooms from $133 per night, four-person family rooms from $165 per night) is the only backpacker place within the historic Rocks district—a modern build alongside the historic setting. Views from the roof terrace (and some of the rooms) rival those of any five-star hotel. This is a gem many would forgo simply because it is a hostel, but the location and facilities are first class and offer dorm rooms as well as private doubles with en suite bathrooms.

$150-250

On a pier underneath the Sydney Harbour Bridge, the **Sebel Pier One Sydney Harbour** (11 Hickson Rd., tel. 02/8298-9999, www.sebelpierone.com.au, from $221) offers some of the best views in town. Minimalist rooms, decorated mostly in white with comfy couches and select art work, mostly photography, are designed to make the most of the views either across the harbor and Luna Park or of the bridge and The Rocks. The Sebel Suite even features an egg-shaped free-standing bath overlooking the harbor.

Dating back to the early 1800s, **The Russell Hotel** (143A George St., tel. 02/9241-3543, www.therussell.com.au, from $154) just off Nurses Walk is an attractive historic hotel full of character and history. Located on a street corner with a small turret above the entrance, it has many period features and quirky room layouts to accommodate its shape. Accommodations vary from a tiny single room with shared bathroom to a family-sized room with en suite facilities, with each room furnished uniquely, suiting its shape and with plenty of architectural and decoration features, from window seats to ceiling plaster roses. It all makes for a charming home away from home in a handy location.

Opposite Harbour Rocks Hotel, **Rendezvous Hotel Sydney The Rocks** (75 Harrington St., tel. 02/9251-6711, www.rendezvoushotels.com, from $230, terraces $360) is a little gem, offering basic and compact studios and larger apartments with and without harbor views. The modern glass entrance belies the fact that the hotel also includes small historic terraced houses next door to the main hotel with a living and entertaining area on the ground floor and bedroom and bathroom upstairs. The decor is modern, the views amazing, and the hotel has a small but enjoyable pool.

Over $250

With understated elegance, luxury, and some of the best views to be had in Sydney, the ★ **Park Hyatt Sydney** (7 Hickson Rd., The Rocks, tel. 02/9256-1234, www.sydney.park.hyatt.com, from $910) delivers and makes the most of all of it. The building itself is modern and not necessarily special, but the location cannot be beaten. You can get an Opera View room that would make pulling the curtains closed a crime. Swim in the stunning rooftop pool overlooking the harbor, the bridge, and the opera house, or enjoy an iconic afternoon tea with champagne, feeling part of Sydney high society. And you'll probably bump into some celebrities in the gym. This is a gorgeous property in a gorgeous location.

The views at the **Shangri-La Hotel** (176 Cumberland St., tel. 02/9250-6000, www.shangri-la.com/sydney, from $355) could hardly get any better. This large skyscraper on Sydney's skyline overlooks The Rocks as well as the harbor, the bridge, and the opera house. Add to that elegant understated hues of brown, tasteful interior decor, spacious rooms with dark-wood furnishings and marble bathrooms, and attentive staff, and you really feel special staying here.

In a beautiful historic Georgian-style building brought back to life, the stunning lobby at the **Harbour Rocks Hotel** (34 Harrington St., tel. 02/8220-9999, www.harbourrocks.com.au, from $349), with its high atrium, welcomes you with soft couches and a wall full of books. The rooms are decorated in elegant browns and have painted brick walls, with exposed brick also featuring in the restaurants. History is palpable throughout the building, built in 1887 on roughly the site of Sydney's first hospital. It's a perfect fit for its perfect location in the heart of The Rocks.

Plush luxury with chintz curtains and comfortable chairs and couches marks **The Langham Hotel Sydney** (89-113 Kent St., tel. 02/9256-2222, http://sydney.

langhamhotels.com.au, from $285) as a traditionally indulgent stay. The colonial-style modern building is decorated with plush luxury in mind. Rooms feature big soft beds and plenty of frilly cushions, linen chests, and all things comfy. The bathrooms and expansive indoor pool, though, are all modern marble, large and extravagant.

CENTRAL BUSINESS DISTRICT (CBD)
Under $150

On the western side of the CBD's main drag, George Street, the ★ **Travelodge Wynyard** (7-9 York St., tel. 02/9274-1222, from $129) is close to the attractions of The Rocks, Circular Quay, and the shops on George Street, and near the train stop of Wynyard, which connects you to the rest of Sydney with ease. Rooms are in understated hues with an abstract print as a splash of color, and they feature a small desk and coffee- and tea-making facilities. As compared to some lower budget stays, this hotel offers a number of amenities: a gym, in-house breakfast, lunch and dinner options, a lobby bar, and in-house laundry.

The **Park Regis City Centre** (27 Park St., tel. 02/9267-6511, www.parkregiscitycentre.com.au, from $144) is a functional hotel without frills, but it boasts a great location and is perfect for simply crashing at night and saving the travel budget for more exciting things. Rooms range from extremely compact (don't opt for the Express Room unless you are a tiny person who travels extremely light) to rather nice, spacious with colored feature walls decorated with modern abstract prints, and views across the city. Amenities include a rooftop pool and a gym, and the hotel delivers well for the price.

Although first impressions may not necessarily be the best, judging by the drab and nondescript outside and the small lobby, the rooms in the ★ **Best Western Plus Hotel Stellar** (4 Wentworth Ave., tel. 02/9264-9754, www.hotelstellar.com, from $130) are spacious, clean, and decorated in an attractive modern style. Small kitchenettes offer the ease of making a coffee in the room or reheating a take-out meal in the microwave, and you simply cannot beat the location. On the corner of Hyde Park and Oxford Street, it's 1.6 kilometers (a 10-minute walk) from Circular Quay and within skipping distance of the shops and sights of the CBD, and 2.1 kilometers from trendy Paddington. There is a bar downstairs.

The **Hotel Coronation** (7 Park St., tel. 02/9266-3100, www.hotelcoronation.com.au, from $109) is basic and simple, with rooms that (apart from the suites) are on the compact side. Being a skip away from the city's shops and sights, this hotel offers location over luxury, and for the location, the prices are great. The large and popular bar downstairs could be a positive or negative point, depending on when you are staying and your demographic, with sleep bound to be somewhat disrupted during weekend nights but much quieter midweek.

$150-250

The fashionable ★ **Establishment Hotel** (5 Bridge Ln., tel. 02/9240-3100, http://merivale.com.au, from $249), in a former warehouse, has 31 sleek and contemporary rooms, all with high ceilings and marble or bluestone baths. Interiors are a mix of colonial heritage and modern with two design schemes: one Japanese-influenced with dramatic black-stained wooden floors, the other decorated in bleached oak and muted fabrics. It is part of a small entertainment complex that is a hub for cool Sydneysiders; the **Hemmesphere Lounge, Tank Club,** and **Gin Garden** are always busy, and chef Peter Doyle has won plenty of accolades for his innovative take on modern Australian cuisine at **Est.** restaurant.

Right on Hyde Park, along chic Elizabeth Street with the museums and Macquarie Street historic sites a brief saunter away, the **Sheraton on the Park** (161 Elizabeth St., tel. 02/9286-6000, www.sheratonontheparksydney.com, from $199) is perfectly placed. Rooms range from simple rooms city-side (no views to speak of) to suites overlooking the park and the harbor in the distance. All are spacious, modern, and comfortable, and the hotel, for a worldwide chain, is individual and inviting. A rooftop pool, health spa, gym, bars and restaurants, plus the Sheraton Club level, make it a great stay at a really convenient location.

With only 36 rooms, the **Park8 Hotel** (185 Castlereagh St., tel. 02/9283-2488, www.park8.com.au, from $209) feels like a private residence rather than an inner city hotel. A Victorian multistory on a corner just by Hyde Park, this little boutique hotel is within easy walking distance of the city shops and sights. Rooms are small but comfortable, with a modern understated decor in hues of gray with the splash of color being a rug or cushions, and there is the option of a split-level two-bed apartment with kitchenette and separate living area.

If you are an Art Deco fan, ★ **The Grace Hotel** (77 York St., tel. 02/9272-6888, www.gracehotel.com.au, from $189) is for you. Located in the iconic Grace Building, designed by Morrow & Gordon and built by Kell & Rigby during the late 1920s, it was opened in 1930 by Grace Brothers, the Australian department store magnates, as their headquarters, and the exterior and the grand lobby are fine examples of the period. The rooms themselves have been renovated in elegant hues of brown and olive, with clean modern furniture befitting the building.

The Grace Hotel

Over $250

Right in the center of the city, the flamboyant, quirky, and thoroughly decadently modern **QT Hotel** (49 Market St., tel. 02/8262-0000, www.qtsydney.com.au, from $450) does not fit into any general hotel category. Entering the hotel feels like stepping into a movie full of props and dressing up. The building used to be a theater, and the general idea of it is still very much alive. Glitzy and glam Las Vegas meets theatrical Sydney—perfect for those who want to make a short stay in Sydney a unique experience.

The **Sir Stamford at Quay** (93 Macquarie St., tel. 02/9252-4600, www.stamford.com, from $275) offers accommodations brimming with old world luxury in the form of antique furniture, crystal chandeliers, and open fireplaces, and even a Steinway grand piano in the Presidential Suite, together with modern amenities of pool and gym and a superb location. Most Deluxe rooms have French doors opening up to balconies, and even the slightly smaller Superior rooms have antique executive desks. All have superior and elegant but comfortable decor. It all makes for a memorable stay. The well-dressed staff and enormous collection of art are reminiscent of a grand hotel in London, and it might be a little much if you are more the flip-flop type.

Imagine a corner window with views across the Sydney Opera House, Circular Quay, and Sydney Harbour Bridge—it does not come much better than that. The ★ **Four Seasons Sydney** (199 George St., tel. 02/9250-3100, www.fourseasons.com/sydney, from $250) offers a variety of rooms with a variety of views: city view (over George Street), city/harbor views (part city, some harbor), and harbor views (all harbor with both opera house and bridge). The rooms themselves are held in understated muted hues, with sleek furniture, but comfortable and homey. Add to that the Endota spa, the liveried staff holding the doors open for you, and the perfect setting at the end of George Street, just across from Circular Quay by The Rocks, and you have a treat of a stay, which is also great for families. Not only can they use Sydney's largest heated outdoor pool, but the concierge has specialized knowledge of family activities around the city, and the room service menu's kids' selection has been developed with the help of the executive chef's daughter, who chose a few of her favorites. Another great addition is the Executive Club Access to the club lounge, which you can opt for daily, whichever room type you are staying in: For $70 for a single person or $105 per couple per day, you get breakfast, Internet access, all day access to coffee, tea, beautiful savory and sweet snacks, soft drinks, and peace and quiet, making the investment a definite saving if you were considering paying for it all separately.

In the old General Post Office building right in the center of the city, steps from the shops, restaurants, and sights, **The Westin** (1 Martin Pl., tel. 02/8223-1111, www.westin.com, from $246) gives you the best of two worlds: rooms located in the old post office building, and rooms in the modern tower above the old GPO, offering you the choice of either super modern luxury rooms or heritage rooms with high ceilings, rounded windows, and older decor and features. It is a large hotel, but well organized with plenty of great restaurants and bars on the premises and even a small museum exhibit of the old Tank Stream in the basement. Whichever you opt for, all rooms are comfortable, with modern amenities, and some of the ones higher up have great views.

At the Circular Quay end of bustling Pitt Street, steps away from the ferries and train connections across Sydney and the restaurants and bars along Bridge Street, the **Sydney Harbour Marriott Hotel at Circular Quay** (30 Pitt St., tel. 02/9259-7000, www.marriott.com.au/Sydney-Hotel, from $279) is a large, comfortable, and perfectly positioned option. The guest rooms are elegant and stylish, more so than the lobby would suggest, and the higher rooms have stunning views across the harbor.

DARLING HARBOUR AND HAYMARKET
Under $150

★ **Metro Hotel Sydney Central** (431-439 Pitt St., Haymarket, tel. 02/9281-6999, www.metrohotels.com.au, from $130) is within walking distance of the CBD, Haymarket, and Darling Harbour, and a stone's throw from the central train station, making it a perfect hub for the city and surroundings. The hotel is also on the pickup list for most bus tours around and out of Sydney. The rooms are spacious, clean, and comfortable and surprisingly quiet considering the closeness of the Capitol Theatre opposite and the many bars and little Asian eateries nearby. This is a great, affordable option for inner Sydney.

Simple and basic, but in a location surrounded by the Darling Harbour restaurants, **Ibis Sydney King Street Wharf** (22 Shelley St., King Street Wharf, Darling Harbour, tel. 02/8243-0700, from $111) is a place to sleep after a day's worth of sightseeing, not necessarily a place to spend hours in your room. Functional and modern, the rooms offer tea- and coffee-making facilities and a small refrigerator, plus there's a bar downstairs.

With a bustling location, **The Woolbrokers at Darling Harbour** (22 Allen St., Pyrmont, tel. 02/9552-4773, standard single rooms from $69, double from $85) is an old-fashioned hostel, with old-fashioned furniture making it much cozier than most. Room options range from single with shared baths, en suite rooms, and family rooms to group rooms sleeping up to eight with bunks included. The accommodations are basic, but all rooms are outfitted with TVs, tea- and coffee-making facilities, and a fridge. Features include breakfast rooms (breakfast $7.50), a courtyard, and guest laundry.

$150-250

The large 525-room **Novotel Darling Harbour** (100 Murray St., Darling Harbour, tel. 02/9934-0000, www.noveldarlingharbour.com.au, from $209) dominates the harbor's skyline and offers everything you'd expect from a global chain. There are various restaurants, a gym, pool, tennis courts, and a wide selection of rooms from single to spacious two-level loft suites with a variety of views, with the one across Darling Harbour being so good that you won't want to go out at night. The rooms themselves are of clean modern decor, hues of beige, brown, and orange, with a small desk and comfy chair. Within a two-minute walk of all the nearby attractions and a mere 10 minutes from the city center, this is a family-friendly (with regular family discounted offers) and comfortable stay.

Australia's largest hotel, with 683 rooms, the **Four Points by Sheraton Sydney** (161 Sussex St., Darling Harbour, tel. 02/9290-4000, www.fourpointssydney.com, from $175) is located between Darling Harbour and the CBD, making it easy to access both within minutes. And it being the large hotel and chain it is, you get all the conveniences only a hotel that size can offer, barring perhaps the personal touch. Rooms are simply furnished with a lot of wood veneer and fresh turquoise accents—simple and functional, nothing plush. It's a business and leisure hotel, so you also get large meeting and conference venues, a pub, a bar, and a buffet-style restaurant, plus a leisure center, slick service, contemporary rooms, and location.

The self-contained ★ **Oaks Goldsborough Apartments** (243 Pyrmont St., Darling Harbour, tel. 02/8586-2500, www.oakshotelsresorts.com, $109 for a studio to $315 for a two-bed executive apartment with harbor view) are located very conveniently next to Darling Harbour, a five-minute walk into the CBD. The vast historic red-brick building, built in 1883, is an old wool store that has been converted into modern apartments with kitchens fully equipped with all utilities, making this a great option for longer-term stays and families.

Over $250

The Darling (The Star, 80 Pyrmont St., Pyrmont, tel. 02/9777-9000, www.thedarling.com.au, from $309), named one of the 60 best new hotels in the world in 2012 by *Condé Nast Traveler*, is part of The Star, a luxury development with shopping, casino, spa, restaurants, and accommodations at the end of Darling Harbour. The modern glass building sits just off the residential area of Pyrmont, and the understated exterior belies the sumptuous interior. Accommodation options range from the standard 35-square-meter Darling rooms upwards to the penthouse, each with distinctive designs and decor, all luxurious. The penthouse is simply mind-blowing, with amazing views through the floor-to-ceiling windows. Very modern in-room technology operates everything from the blinds to the TV to the wake-up calls. Features include adult-only floors, Molton Brown cosmetic goodies, and a level of service that puts many other top hotels to shame.

Also part of The Star development, in the same shiny glass tower, the **Astral Tower** (The Star, 80 Pyrmont St., Pyrmont, tel. 02/9777-9000, www.star.com.au, from $309) offers one- to three-bedroom apartments, easy access to all The Star facilities, and a choice of views across the harbor or the city. The rooms are in understatedly elegant brown and gray hues with natural wood accents and plush carpets; many have window seats to make the most of the views. Considering the closeness to restaurants and the casino, the hotel has a strict no-party policy and monitors alcohol consumption, to ensure guests get the rest they deserve.

The ★ **1888 Hotel** (139 Murray St., Pyrmont, tel. 1800/818-880, www.1888hotel.com.au, from $179) has reached some fame as reportedly the first Instagram hotel in the world, encouraging guest to post pictures of the chic interior and offering a "selfie" space. The hotel is certainly modern and combines the heritage setting well with its trendy outlook. The imposing brick building still has many of the original 1888 features, such as three-meter-high ceilings in the rooms, large exposed beams and bare brickwork, and large old windows; even the sign 1888 on the outside had to remain in place, as it is a listed building. Add to that minimalist modern furniture and artwork, and the combination works surprisingly well. Rooms range from tiny (Shoebox, 15 square meters) to relatively roomy (The Attic, 30 square meters inside and 17 square meters on an outdoor patio), but all have smart interiors and are equipped with free Wi-Fi, media hubs, and free access to the large swimming pool at the Ian Thorpe Aquatic Centre across the road. A great and unusual place.

KINGS CROSS AND DARLINGHURST
Under $150

Next door to the popular celebrity-chef-owned Hugo's Restaurant in Kings Cross, **The Bayswater** (17 Bayswater Rd., Kings Cross, tel. 02/8070-0100, www.sydneylodges.com, from $130) offers chic, clean-cut accommodations in a bustling hub, just around the corner from the big Coke sign. It might be a little noisy on weekends, but you're probably joining the revelers anyway.

The Challis Lodge (21-23 Challis Ave., Potts Point, tel. 02/9358-5422, www.sydneylodges.com, from $65) is a basic guesthouse that offers simple and modern rooms with an option of shared or en suite bathroom facilities, a communal kitchen, and laundry facilities, in a lovely period building in the colonial style, complete with arched and columned wrap-around verandas.

$150-250

Formerly The Storrier, **Quest Potts Point** (15 Springfield Ave., Kings Cross, tel. 02/8988-6999, www.questapartments.com.au, petite studio from $150) was inspired by contemporary Australian artist Tim Storrier. This little apartment hotel is tucked in a lane a couple of hops from Macleay Street, the bustling Kings Cross main thoroughfare. The snazzy interior includes monochrome upholstery, striped lampshades, and unusual pieces of art, and a rooftop terrace has great views across the city. The studios are small but adequate—a good value.

In a renovated heritage building dating back to 1892, **Simpsons of Potts Point** (8 Challis Ave., Potts Point, tel. 02/9356-2199, www.simpsonshotel.com, from $235) was originally known as Killountan and consists of two adjoining buildings: the main house at the front and a servants' wing at the rear. A meandering big brick and timber house with myriad gables, nooks, and crannies, its style is Victorian cum Arts and Crafts. In the heart of chic residential area Potts Point, yet a mere five-minute walk from bustling Kings Cross, this is an accommodation option that is secluded and private. Homey rooms have a personal touch, each one decorated individually and cozy, with bedspreads, armchairs, and heritage-style decor, and you won't want to leave the old-fashioned library/drawing room, which has an open fire in winter.

Over $250

A Victorian townhouse in a quiet residential area, the historic exterior of the ★ **Medusa Hotel** (267 Darlinghurst Rd., Darlinghurst, tel. 02/3991-1000, www.medusa.com.au, from $310) belies its funky and luxurious interior. The little boutique hotel's 18 rooms range from Grand Rooms in the old part of the building, with high ceilings and larger sizes, to more compact rooms in the back. Either way, the rooms are a mix of contemporary and historic, with great pieces of colorful, modern furniture coupled with the architectural character of the original building. Individual, artfully designed, and full of character, the Medusa offers an individual stay close to the city and the hub of Kings Cross.

The Contemporary (Surrey St.,

Darlinghurst, tel. 02/9698-4661, www.tct-sydneyaccommodation.com.au, from $295 per night for a three-night stay) is one of three properties dotted throughout Sydney's central suburbs developed by the so-called "tastemaker of Sydney," Geoff Clark. The one-off boutique one-bedroom apartments are designed individually and tastefully, like someone's private home. Rooms are available on a three-night-minimum basis, unless you are willing to pay an inflated price for one night (from $475). The Contemporary has charcoal painted walls full of quirky artwork, and rooms are accented with wooden tables, seedpod-like lamps, earthy African-style rugs and cushions, and even the odd trunk and suitcase to complete the tasteful "travel-the-world" theme of its decor. Small, but big enough to sleep two, each apartment has a tiny kitchen and amenities in the bathroom. Even a beach towel and picnic basket are provided. This is a home away from home with restaurants and cafés within easy walking distance.

PADDINGTON
Under $150

The Arts Hotel (21 Oxford St., tel. 02/9361-0211, www.arthotel.com.au, from $134) is perfectly located for access to Paddington, Darlinghurst, and, via bus, the CBD and Bondi. Small, modern, and simply decorated, this hotel is affordable and handy for a brief city break.

Paddington is a mostly residential area, and the charm lies often behind the individual buildings you normally can't get access to, so why not rent a vacation property and stay right among those who live here? **HomeAway** (www.homeaway.com.au, from $100 per night) offers properties ranging from studio apartments to gorgeous Victorian terraces, sleeping between two to more than 10 people, depending on the property.

$150-250

★ **Kathryn's on Queen** (20 Queen St., 02/9327-4535, www.kathryns.com.au, from $180) is a lovely little boutique bed-and-breakfast in a heritage-listed Victorian terrace, situated a stone's throw from the fashion district in Paddington. The rooms are light and airy, decorated in the shabby chic style: comfortable, stylish, and lovingly worn furniture that complements the setting. Le Attic overlooks the city's skyline and the harbor bridge from the top of the building, while Le Grand looks out on Queen Street and has its own balcony and marble fireplace. Both have private bathrooms.

★ **The Hughenden** (14 Queens St., Woollahra, tel. 02/9363-4863, www.thehughenden.com.au, from $158) is in a rambling white Victorian villa built in the 1870s, and it embraces both the antique features and the slight shabbiness that comes with old buildings. Many rooms, however, have been renovated, so fear not. Antique furniture, matching curtains and bedcovers, cushions, and old-fashioned bedside lamps make the rooms cozy and in keeping with the style of the house. This is a pet-friendly hotel, so if you don't want to risk hairs in your room, ask for a non-pet room. The location is fantastic for Paddington and Centennial Park, and the buses into the CBD and Bondi depart a few steps away.

THE NORTHERN SHORE
Under $150

Falcon Lodge (182 Falcon St., North Sydney, tel. 02/9955-2358, www.falconlodge.com.au, from $41), in a terrace of Federation buildings, offers a range of very simple rooms, some with shared bathroom facilities, others en suite. Select rooms have a small kitchenette where you can prepare basic meals. A shared kitchen, laundry facilities, weekly linen service, and free Wi-Fi make this popular with longer-stay guests and families on a budget.

A campsite/caravan park, **Lane Cove River Tourist Park** (Plassey Rd., Macquarie Park, tel. 02/9888-9133, lccp@environment.nsw.gov.au, from $37 for an unpowered site), right in the heart of Lane Cove National Park, is shady and restful and offers the usual amenities, such as shared bathroom blocks, laundry facilities, camp kitchen, a recreation room with a TV, and a pool. A kiosk sells basic supplies, and there's public transport from North Ryde Station, some 700 meters from the site.

$150-250

Vibe Hotel North Sydney (88 Alfred St., North Sydney, tel. 02/8272-3300, www.vibehotels.com.au, from $143) is just a skip away from Milsons Point train station and a brief stroll from the ferry stop, connecting you with Sydney's CBD and its attractions within easy public transport reach of 5-10 minutes, yet the prices at this sleek modern hotel seem much farther away from the city center. The rooms all offer reasonable space with a small seating area, and many have a view across the harbor. The hotel has its own pool (overlooking pretty Lavender Bay) and a sauna, and also offers free access to the Olympic swimming pool nearby and packages to Luna Park.

Near the ferry point, allowing you access to Sydney within a 10-minute ride, the modern **Harbourside Apartment Hotel** (2a Henry Lawson Ave., McMahons Point, tel. 02/9963-4300, http://harboursideapartments.com.au, studios from $209) offers a variety of accommodations, from studio apartments to one- and two-bedroom apartments. Each can be had without a view or with views across the bridge toward the opera house. All apartments are in neutral earthy tones with light blue accents, modern and elegant furnishings, and, if you opt for a larger apartment, comfy couches and chairs. Except for the studios, the apartments come with full kitchens. A harborside pool, barbecue facilities, guest laundry and dry-cleaning service, a daily paper, and access to the popular **Sails on Lavender Bay** restaurant make this a family friendly and comfortable place to stay, with rates becoming more budget friendly if you are staying a longer term, such as 10 days.

In the suburbs, ★ **Cremorne Point Manor** (6 Cremorne Rd., Cremorne Point, www.cremornepointmanor.com.au, tel. 02/9953-7899, from $75 for single room with shared shower to $259 for en suite King Spa suite) is a fully restored late 1800s federation-style double-story villa with balustrade balconies and verandas, less than a 10-minute ferry ride from the CBD, with great views from some rooms and the roof terrace. Rooms are simply furnished but with nice touches such as cushions and bedspreads; it's not high quality furniture, but it's functional. At this family-run boutique place, it is the small details that make this special: a robe and slippers, little toiletries in the bathrooms, and lovely art collected from around the world set in beautiful frames. Nooks and crannies where you can sit with a cup of tea and a book make this a great place away from Sydney, yet near to Sydney.

Over $250

★ **Roar and Snore** (Bradleys Head Rd., Mosman, tel. 02/9978-4791, www.taronga.org.au/roarandsnore, weekdays from $288 adult, $184.50 child, weekends from $320 adult, $205 child, includes all meals and drinks, strictly no BYO) is the best place to sleep for a night, if you have kids or you are one at heart. You're right in the zoo, with amazing views across the harbor to the bridge and opera house with the Sydney skyline on the horizon, and the animals are just outside the (small) fence surrounding the camp. And it *is* camping. The tents are spacious, with two or three beds in them, but that is pretty much it, although the site offers everything you'll need (all amenities, beds, linens, etc., are provided). You obviously have access to the zoo, and you will meet a "creature" (depending on whose turn it is) and get a behind-the-scenes look. Plus there's tea and nibbles upon arrival, dinner, and a light breakfast before you leave.

THE BEACHES
Bondi

On the hill behind the Iceberg swimming pool, halfway to Tamarama Beach, the clean and friendly ★ **Bondi Beachouse YHA** (63 Fletcher St., Bondi Beach, tel. 02/9365-2088, www.yha.com.au, beds from $30) is still within easy walking distance of the two beaches and all the action down on Bondi. The accommodations are mostly shared rooms, but there are also some double rooms with private bathrooms (from $90). The hostel has a communal kitchen, barbecue, free snorkeling gear, and surfboards for hire. A small supermarket is just round the corner, and there are plenty of backpacker pubs and eateries nearby.

Two minutes from the beach and the shops, the spacious apartments at **Adina Bondi Beach** (69-73 Hall St., Bondi Beach, tel. 02/9300-4800, www.adinahotels.com.au, studio from $249) are decorated in sandy tones, complemented by light turquoise and blues and timber accents, reflecting their famous location. Ranging from studios to one- to three-bedroom apartments, all have balconies, kitchens, and laundry and living areas, and the hotel offers a grocery delivery service. Interconnecting rooms make it easy to expand the apartments to a size you need.

You can't get any more central than **Ravesi's Hotel** (118 Campbell Parade, Bondi Beach, tel. 02/9365-4422, www.ravesis.com.au, from $269). Overlooking the beach and promenade, Ravesi's Hotel is mostly a restaurant plus wine and cocktail bar on two levels. But 12 individual rooms have stylish half-rounded windows (alas, only a couple overlook the seafront), with modern and quite masculine decor: walls in dark chocolate hues and golden-brown accents set with pieces of art and cushions. The rooms offer a more urban than beach experience, but if you want to be where Bondi is happening, this is it.

Coogee

A large hotel resort overlooking lovely Coogee Beach, the **Crowne Plaza Coogee Beach** (242 Arden St., Coogee, tel. 02/9315-7600, www.crowneplaza.com, from $208) offers all the amenities and facilities you'd ask for in a well-known chain hotel. There are several dining options, a health club, and access to several nearby pools, and the beach is just across the road. Contemporary in design, the rooms are open and airy, and all offer a comfortable chair and desk area, as well as in-room dining. Guests in the ocean-view rooms have been known to see whales from their balcony.

Tamarama

The **Tama Beach House** (22 Deliview St., Tamarama, tel. 02/9365-0259, http://tamabeach.com, from $98) is divided into four separate apartments, which offer a private self-contained vacation experience. The house itself is a large white modern building with the pool, and the inside is fresh and beachy, with lots of white and turquoise and wood befitting the summery location. A good-size pool-view studio on the ground floor opens to the paved pool area and has a kitchen, living area, and free Wi-Fi. The ocean-view apartment (from $150) has two bedrooms and offers stunning views across the little Tamarama Beach, just a 20-minute walk from Bondi along the gorgeous beachfront walk. A small but airy pool-view studio has the shower in the kitchen area, and a pool-view apartment includes a separate bedroom, living and dining area, plus outside seating.

Manly

From dorm rooms to private en suite rooms, the **Manly Boardrider** (63 The Corso, Manly, tel. 02/9977-6677, www.boardrider.com.au, from $30 for a dorm bed, $125 for deluxe room with bathroom) is a hostel cum motel, but a place to party rather than sleep. Modern, basic, and clean, it is the destination for backpackers in Manly. It's right there on the Corso, among the pubs, nightclubs, and all the action. There are daily organized activities ranging from beach volleyball to pub crawls, from quiz nights to barbecues. Never a dull—or quiet—moment.

Right out on the point where Sydney Harbour meets the Tasman Sea, ★ **Q Station** (1 North Head Scenic Dr., Manly, tel. 02/9466-1500, www.qstation.com.au, from $133) is an idyllic spot right in the Sydney Harbour National Park. This former quarantine station dates back to 1832, with original historic buildings still dotted around the site. A selection of colonial-style, beautifully restored, and in places modern main buildings, together with a handful of renovated historic cottages, nestle in the green surroundings. Wrap-around verandas and balconies, together with a lot of decking, and wood used in the interior give the space a light and airy atmosphere. This hotel resort is a destination in itself, with Sydney being a place you visit on day trips. Here you go for walks, snorkel, kayak, or simply enjoy sitting on the terrace and watching the myriad boats on the harbor. It offers a good deal of variety—heritage rooms, deluxe harbor-view rooms, private and secluded retreat suites, and the separate historic cottages in the national park. There are restaurants and bars, and a concierge service organizes your day trips for you, should you really want to leave.

The Sebel Manly Beach (8-13 S. Steyne, Manly, tel. 02/9977-8866, www.accorhotels.com, from $233) is on the beachfront at Manly, 30 minutes from Sydney's CBD by fast ferry. The 83 spacious rooms in the light and modern building dominated by large windows have private balconies to make the most of the views. The rooms are simply and tastefully decorated, in light earthy colors. A casual beachside restaurant offers anything from breakfast through to a glass of wine over dinner. There is a pool and sauna, and the hotel offers baby-sitting on request.

The beachfront **Novotel Sydney Manly Pacific** (55 N. Steyne, Manly, tel. 02/9977-7666, www.novotelmanlypacific.com.au, from $242) is a sister to the Novotel Darling Harbour, but on a smaller scale. The modern building is functional, with 213 guest rooms ranging from single rooms to family rooms and two-bedroom suites. The rooms are spacious, in beige and brown tones—simple but comfortable. This is a modern "all singing and dancing" hotel of a chain that knows what it's doing when it comes to around-the-world guest services and facilities, with several bars and restaurants and a pool. There's also a play center for the kids and plenty of special family-friendly offers.

Food

THE ROCKS AND CIRCULAR QUAY

Often voted the best restaurant in Australia, ★ **Quay** (Upper Level, Overseas Passenger Terminal, The Rocks, tel. 02/9251-5600, www.quay.com.au, lunch Tues.-Fri. noon-2:30pm, dinner daily 6pm-10pm, three-course lunch menu from $130, four-course dinner menu from $175) also comes with the best views. Next to Sydney Harbour Bridge, looking across to the Sydney Opera House, this modern glass-encased eatery by celebrity chef Peter Gilmore delights with simply stunning dishes. You will recognize the names of most of the ingredients, but what the chef does with them is pretty much out of this world. Your steak, for example, is prepared with grains and miso, your fish would be a Tasmanian trumpeter with smoked oyster crackling, and for dessert you must have the snow-egg, which you crack open to reveal custardy goodness inside. This treat for all the senses, while expensive, is truly worth it.

On a corner plot in the heart of The Rocks, ★ **Baroque** (Bushells Pl., 88 George St., tel. 02/9241-4811, www.baroquebistro.com.au, daily 8am-3pm, fine dining Thurs.-Sat. 6pm-late) is a great place to sit outside and watch the bustling life around you while munching on pan-roasted barramundi, Australia's best-loved fish, with globe artichoke and zucchini ($26). If you are less hungry, a simple croque monsieur might do ($17). Baroque is split into a daytime bistro and a nighttime fine dining restaurant and wine bar. Come for dinner in the copper-accented modern indoor setting with open kitchen, and be wowed by the French chef's beautifully constructed and prepared plates, a fusion of French and modern Australian cuisine. The dishes usually look too pretty to eat, but if you have to, try something innovative, such as the beetroot starter with hay and goat curd, followed by the quinoa-encrusted lamb loin with onion puree and olive jus (mains $38).

Step out of Sydney and straight into Paris at **Ananas** (18 Argyle St., The Rocks, tel. 02/9259-5668, www.ananas.com.au, lunch Mon.-Fri. noon-3pm, dinner Mon.-Wed. 6pm-midnight, Thurs.-Sat. 6pm-3am, bar open Mon.-Fri. from noon, Sat. from 4pm, mains $37). The Art Deco interior is as chic as the exposed brick of this heritage building, and the food is *délicieuse,* including traditional steak frites, oysters shucked to order, a superb wild mushroom pappardelle, and a hint of truffle lingering in the air. Dress up, grab a champagne flute, and enjoy being with the young and beautiful of Sydney. Stay until the morning. Reportedly the urinals are somewhat scandalous—red-lipped, like an open mouth (the author apologizes for not being allowed a close look to check that statement).

Australia is known for its steaks on the barbecue, and at **Phillip's Foote Restaurant** (101 George St., The Rocks, tel. 02/9241-1485, www.phillipsfoote.com.au, Mon.-Sat. noon-midnight, Sun. noon-10pm) that is exactly what you get. You buy your steak at the counter, take it to the communal barbecue outside in the yard by the little lane called Suez Canal, and you cook the steak to your liking. Help yourself from the salad bar, top up with sauces and bread, and that's that. If you think $32 for a steak, salad, potatoes, and bread is a lot considering you are doing the cooking and serving yourself, maybe you're right, but it is fun, and you'll have a new experience—and a decent steak. There are also fish and chicken options. The restaurant itself is an unpretentious old-fashioned pub, absolutely no frills, but cooking a steak on the barbie with some mates—you don't get more Aussie than that.

The Vintage Café (3 Nurses Walk, The Rocks, tel. 02/9252-2055, www.vintagecafe.com.au, Mon.-Wed. 10:30am-4:30pm, Thurs.-Fri. 10:30am-9:30pm, Sat.-Sun. 9am-9:30pm) is ideal for a lunchtime snack. You can choose from tapas or various sharing plates, with mostly Mediterranean food options. Tapas are around $11 per plate; paella for two is $58. The café is in a great building with exposed bricks and beams, quirky roofing, and a historic setting. The lovely wood balcony is perfect for dining alfresco.

Pony Dining (corner Kendall Ln. and Argyle St., The Rocks, tel. 02/9252-7767, www.ponydining.com.au, daily noon-3pm) is a contemporary and relaxed place famed for its "butchers block" food, such as steaks (800-gram T-bone to share, $85) and its Pony on a Bun burgers ($18.50). The decor of exposed brick and pony-skin wall coverings, together with the gleaming kitchen busy with chefs plying their trade, is a great setting. Sitting outside on the wooden deck allows you to people-watch while you eat.

Guylian Belgian Chocolate Café (91 George St., The Rocks, tel. 02/8274-7500, Sun.-Thurs. 8am-11pm, Fri.-Sat. 8am-midnight) offers lunchtime specials for $12.50 for a baguette sandwich and a glass of wine—but really you'd come here for the hot chocolate ($7.50) and the Belgian waffles that indulgently come with chocolate dip and ice cream ($15). And you can indulge nearly all night long, too. Just add a glass of wine to your waffle and enjoy the charming heritage building and surroundings.

Hidden downstairs from Sydney Visitor Centre and opposite The Rocks Discovery Museum, ★ **The Fine Food Store** (The Rocks Centre, corner Kendall Ln. and Mill Ln., tel. 02/9252-1196, Mon.-Sat. 7am-5pm, Sun. 7:30am-5pm), a deli-cum-coffee shop, serves seriously delicious salads and sandwiches. The setting is relaxed, the staff lovely, and if you sit by the table benches at the window you can peek out on the cobbled lane and watch the people go by. Don't leave without trying the toasted beetroot, walnut, and cheese sandwich ($9.50)—have it with an iced tea for perfection.

CENTRAL BUSINESS DISTRICT (CBD)

The award-winning, highly acclaimed ★ **Tetsuya's** (529 Kent St., tel. 02/9267-2900, www.tetsuyas.com, dinner Tues.-Fri. from 6pm, lunch Sat. from noon, dinner Sat. from 6:30pm, 10-course degustation menu without drinks $220 pp) is a true treat, one that comes with a price tag but also provides a priceless experience. The restaurant itself is a cross between a Japanese shrine and an art gallery, complete with zen garden, and chef Tetsuya is known for his philosophy of using natural and in-season ingredients, enhanced by traditional French cuisine techniques, and his degustation menu is a journey through the world's best ingredients, with a leaning toward the Japanese cuisine, but with plenty of courses that are fusion or truly international. Try the tea-smoked quail breast or confit of ocean trout, along with the white peaches with almond milk ice cream for dessert.

Modern and glass-encased with a simply elegant interior, **Aria** (1 Macquarie St., tel. 02/9252-2555, www.ariarestaurant.com, Mon.-Fri. noon-2:30pm and 5:30pm-11pm, Sat. 5pm-11pm, Sun. 6pm-10pm, pre-theater menu 5:30pm-7pm, one-course lunch $46, two-course lunch $74, two-course dinner from $105) boasts an award-winning celebrity chef. The views will make you forget the food in front of you. At probably the most memorable address in the city, right at the beginning of historic Macquarie Street, by the opera house, Circular Quay, and the bridge, Aria produces plates of food that look as if they come straight from an art gallery. Even if you think you know the ingredient, you'll be surprised at the new take on it, so even if you go for an old favorite, you'll be trying something new. The modern Australian cuisine offers tidbits such as spanner crab mayonnaise with pine nuts, nasturtium, and persimmon; truffled baby cabbage with king brown oyster mushrooms and chestnuts; and black sesame parfait with passionfruit jelly. Tempted?

As the name suggests, the main ingredient at ★ **The Woods** (199 George St., Four Seasons Hotel, tel. 02/9250-3160, lunch Mon.-Fri. noon-2:30pm, dinner Mon.-Sat. 5:30pm-10:30pm, coffee, drinks, and snacks Mon.-Fri. all day, Sat. from 5:30pm, $38) is wood. Not to eat, but to cook with. Large wood-burning ovens and grills feature different woods each week, anything from olive, grapevine, lemon, orange, apple, or peach wood, all giving special flavors to the ingredients. And it is not just meat that is smoked or cooked over wood. The starter of smoked beetroot with labne and hazelnut is great, and daily specials, such as lamb, are simply gorgeous. The setting, although in the hotel lobby, is discreet and relaxing. The ceiling is scribbled with recipes, there is a herb wall, and little anecdotes are framed between the bottle displays, giving the restaurant an elegant yet quirky feel. The spacious low-benched open kitchen adds to the theater. There is a separate vegetarian menu, with some vegan options, in addition to the daily menu.

Spice Temple (10 Bligh St., tel. 02/8078-1888, www.spicetemple.com.au, lunch Mon.-Sat. noon-3pm, dinner 6pm-11pm, mains $40) is celebrity chef Neil Perry's offering to all things Asian, but without a red-tasseled light shade in sight. Instead you have stylish understated Asian decor, plenty of hanging lights, and terribly chic beaded curtains. This restaurant does stylish, spicy, tasty, beautiful food "with a twist" incredibly well, focusing mostly on regional Chinese cuisine. In the main restaurant opt for delicacies such as a seriously spicy and crispy duck, or the poached chicken and noodle salad. At the bar, however, you've got to try the "burger," a dumpling with pork, pickles, and chili that is positively addictive.

Way up high above Sydney's CBD you can find the **360 Bar & Dining** restaurant (Sydney Tower, Sydney Westfield Centre, between Pitt St. and Castlereagh St., tel. 02/8223-3883, www.360dining.com.au, access via lift on level 4, lunch Mon.-Fri. noon-2pm, dinner daily 5:30pm-9pm, two-course dinner from $75). The 360-degree views are magnificent, especially of the sparkling city at night, which complements the sparkling and showy restaurant setting. The food is stylish modern Australian with all the favorites, such as confit of duck, roasted lamb, and an impressive selection of steaks, plus local fish choices such as hapuka and Tasmanian salmon.

Don't let the name of ★ **The Morrison Bar and Oyster Room** (225 George St., tel. 02/9247-6744, http://themorrison.com.au, Mon.-Fri. 7:30am-late, Sat.-Sun. 11:30am-late) put you off. Yes, there are plenty of fresh oysters, especially at Wednesday's happy hour, when they go for $1 apiece, and you can choose from an oyster library listing the mind-blowing array of the critters. But there are also plenty of other options, such as the fish of the day (for example, a whole John Dory to share, $45), and the duck-fat fries are superb. This wood-paneled, partly old-fashioned, partly hypermodern eatery is a great place to grab a drink and a bite to eat. It's always busy, but not overwhelmingly so, and it makes for a good atmosphere.

A trendy restaurant in the grand setting of Customs House, **Young Alfred** (Customs House, 31 Alfred St., Circular Quay, tel. 02/9251-5192, www.youngalfred.com.au, Mon.-Fri. 7am-late, Sat. noon-10pm) has a mostly modern Italian menu. Try the roasted chicken salad ($18) or the gnocchi with basil, or the delectable fungi risotto ($24) for a treat. It's a popular spot with the workers from the CBD for lunch and after-work drinks, but the buzz adds to the atmosphere.

The tiny little ★ **Portobello Caffe** (East Circular Quay, tel. 02/9247-8548, daily for breakfast, lunch, and dinner) undoubtedly occupies the best spot in the city, right on Circular Quay, on the way to the opera house and overlooking the quay with its busy ferries and the bridge. You'll want to linger here forever. But alas, it is only a place to sit outside and grab a panini ($15) or gelato, while enjoying the views. There's good coffee, too. Next door is the **Sydney Cove Oyster Bar** (East Circular Quay, tel. 02/9247-2937, daily 9am-9pm), like Portobello also a small hut (maybe once a ticket office or security hutch?) with outside seating. Here you get said oysters, chilled lobster (half for $59, whole for $120), caviar, and champagne—appropriate food to accompany the million-dollar view.

Bridge St. Garage Bar and Diner (17-19 Bridge St., CBD, tel. 02/9251-9392, www.bridgestgarage.com.au, Mon.-Tues. noon-5pm, Wed.-Sat. noon-late, burger $19.50, sticky pork ribs $36) is an American style bistro where decadent fare like burgers, fries, and ribs is served on rustic wooden boards. It also offers a huge beer list. A nice combination of chic and comfort, the setting is fantastic, with tiles and open brick, set off by wall murals and large globe lights.

Within the gorgeous renaissance interior of the General Post Office, surrounded by marble, wood, and colonnades, the grand Italian restaurant **Intermezzo** (GPO, Martin's Place, tel. 02/9229-7788, lunch Mon.-Fri. noon-3pm, dinner Mon.-Sat. 6pm-10pm, mains $32) offers style and elegance, together with an award-winning wine list and food experience. There's no pizza here, but instead traditional dishes such as veal roll filled with smoked bocconcini (a mozzarella-like cheese) and pine nuts, and handmade meatballs of pork and veal.

Just one of the food outlets in Hunter Connection, an Asian food court, **Ooh Rice?!** (7-13 Hunter St., CBD, tel. 02/9223-9962, Mon.-Fri. 11am-3pm, dishes around $8.50) specializes in Japanese curry, and it's delicious. If you like Japanese food but are bored with all things sushi and crave something a little more hearty, this is a really cheap and tasty lunch option.

DARLING HARBOUR AND HAYMARKET

At **Zaaffran** (Level 2, 345 Harbourside Shopping Centre, Darling Harbour, tel. 02/9211-8900, www.zaaffran.com, daily noon-9:30pm), on the second level of the Darling Harbour Harbourside complex, the crowd usually is a good mix of tourists and Indian families, always a good sign when you're eating at an Indian restaurant. Established in 1998, this is not your typical Indian restaurant when it comes to looks—it is modern, open, with great views across the harbor—but the food is just as it should be. There are lassis, paneers, curries, nan, and tandoor-cooked meats, and the portions are ample. There is even a biryani pie, which is somewhat unusual, and a Zaaffran specialty.

If only a good steak will do, look no further than **I'm Angus** (The Promenade, Cockle Bay, Darling Harbour, tel. 02/9264-5822, Mon.-Sat. 11:30am-3pm and 5:30pm-10pm, Sun. 11:30am-10pm, steaks around $25). This is a huge and bustling steak house, right on the water's edge, and while it does token foods of other types, steak is the thing you come here for. No excuses. It's what they do best.

Sit by the wharf at **Nick's Seafood Restaurant** (The Promenade, King Street Wharf, tel. 1300/989-989, www.nicks-seafood.com.au, Sun.-Thurs. 11:30am-10pm, Fri.-Sat. 11:30am-11pm, mains $38) and watch the myriad day-tripping boats come and go and visitors from around the world saunter past, all while enjoying the freshest catch of the day prepared to your liking. The interior spills across the wide open sliding doors, merging the restaurant's indoor and outdoor seating and making for an airy atmosphere. Have a huge platter with a variety of seafood to share for the table, or try a grilled fish with a salad. For lunch or dinner, this is a great place to sit and enjoy what the sea around Australia dishes up.

★ **Pump House** (17 Little Pier St., Darling Harbour, tel. 02/8217-4100, www.pumphousebar.com.au, daily noon-11pm, pizza $19) is a microbrewery in a fantastic old building, originally designed and built as a pumping station in 1890 for the Sydney & Suburban Hydraulic Power Company, before times of electricity. Apart from the rather impressive beer and drinks list, the food is simple: pizza, lunch specials such as pumpkin pasta, and steaks, catch of the day fish, and fresh local produce on the dinner menu. An interesting option is the skilled matching of beers to your food to get the most out of both, as recommended by your beer sommelier.

Need a quick and easy Japanese food fix? **Umi Sushi & Udon** (Shop 10/1-25 Harbour St., Darling Harbour, tel. 02/9283-2006, daily 11:30am-10pm) is a large setup with long sushi bars around the preparation areas, but also some tables for a more intimate setting, and outside there's plenty of seating near the Chinese Garden of Friendship. There's excellent miso soup for only $2.50, chicken udon ($11), and sushi such as tuna nigiri at $4.60 each, and even kids' bento boxes ($9.80).

The large **Emperor's Garden Restaurant** (96-100 Hay St., Haymarket, tel. 02/9211-2135, www.emperorsgarden.com.au, daily 7:30am-1:30am) serves decent Cantonese food, but the main draw is the little window to the side of it, on Dixon Street. This is where you get the Emperor's Puffs: delicate small warm puffs of dough filled with custard, sold in a bag at $0.30 each, or four for $1. Just look for the line of patiently waiting people, all day and night—you can't miss it.

KINGS CROSS

★ **Otto Ristorante** (Area 8/6, Cowper Wharf Roadway, Woolloomooloo, tel. 02/9368-7488, www.ottoristorante.com.au, daily noon-10:30pm, mains $35) offers a spectacular setting, by the water underneath the Royal Botanic Gardens and the Art Gallery of NSW, and serves up Italian food with a twist. The restaurant is modern and elegant, yet also relaxing and perfect for an evening out, be it summer or winter (in winter the outside heaters warm the atmosphere to comfortable levels). The food really shines: Try the *crudo di tonno,* butter-soft, thin yellowfin tuna served with miniature pickled cucumber balls and crispy pork crackling; the *pici,* porcini pasta with wild-boar ragout; or play it safe with the fish of the day special. Then end with the rich-but-worth-it white chocolate and hazelnut mousse with peanut butter wafers. Savor the little quirky additions to every meal and the superb presentation, but don't forget to look around you occasionally.

Awarded two hats by the *SMH (Sydney Morning Herald) Good Food Guide 2012-2013*, **Gastro Park** (5 Roslyn St., Kings Cross, tel. 02/8068-1017, www.gastropark.com.au, lunch Thurs.-Sat. from noon, dinner Tues.-Sat. 6pm-late, mains $45) is a self-confessed playground for the tastebuds. You might not expect to find a little gem like this in the backstreets of Kings Cross, but people have been discovering this restaurant with its simple but elegant decor that is at odds with the somewhat eclectic life playing out on the streets nearby. The food (modern Australian) is whimsical, risk-taking, and delicious. The menus change daily, always offering what is fresh and in season. You might have steamed Murray cod with charred white asparagus, or even suckling pig with endive, grapes, carrot, and plum with some caramelized apple skins for dessert.

The restaurant and wine bar **Monopole** (71a Macleay St., Potts Point, tel. 02/9360-4410, www.monopolesydney.com.au, dinner daily from 5pm, lunch Sat.-Sun. noon-around 3pm) is casual yet classy. Sit by the bar or along the long leather couch lining the opposite wall, or indeed grab, if you can, the window seat and watch life go by outside. Monopole's food is modern Australian with a twist, and beautiful. The baby corn on the cob is still dressed in leaves but chargrilled to perfection, and the cress salad is decorated with edible flowers, making it nearly too pretty to eat. Plates to share are around $26 for a selection of various starters, such as cured meats; mains are around $20.

The family-run Italian restaurant **Puntino** (41 Crown St., Woolloomooloo, tel. 02/9331-8566, www.puntino.com.au, lunch Tues.-Fri. noon-3:30pm, dinner Tues.-Sat. 6pm-10:30pm), complete with wooden tables and red-checkered napkins adding to its homey atmosphere, is a perennial favorite of Sydneysiders. Mozzarella *degustazione* platters ($15.50 pp, to share) and black-truffle-infused pasta ($24) make it difficult to leave enough space for the Nutella pizza for dessert.

On first glance it's a mere hot-dog stand by the harbor, but ★ **Harvey Café de Wheels** (corner Cowper Wharf Roadway and Brougham Rd., Woolloomooloo, tel. 02/9357-3074, www.harryscafedewheels.com.au, daily 8:30am-2am, pie $6.20) is really a Sydney legend. Sydney's best hot dogs and savory pies are served up all day until late in the night, making it perfect for snacks, lunch, something on the run, or, especially, a perfect midnight snack after a few drinks in the nearby bars.

Bar Coluzzi (322 Victoria St., Kings Cross, tel. 02/9380-5420, daily 10am-2pm) is a tiny roadside coffee shop easily overlooked if it weren't for the assortment of people sitting on wooden stumps and crates on the pavement slurping their coffees. Typically Italian, this little place oozes the kind of atmosphere you have in a side alley of Rome: crowded with coffee drinkers, all talking at once, yet somebody will be sitting quietly reading a book, with no thought given to the decor of the place bar the stools and tables. Nobody cared about interior design here, and people gladly share their wooden pallets and stools with other people stopping for a brief interlude. Stay for breakfast or lunch (they do a nice home-made lasagna), but definitely have a coffee.

PADDINGTON

Hidden in a quaint backyard, little **Jackies Café** (1c Glenmore Rd., off Oxford St., Paddington, tel. 02/9380-9818, www.jackies-cafe.com.au, daily 8am-3:30pm, breakfast $18) is perfect for a lazy breakfast or a light fresh lunch and a glass of bubbles after shopping on trendy Oxford Street. The café offers outdoor and indoor seating, from cozy tables to communal benches where you might have to share the Sunday papers with your neighbor. The food has more than a hint of Italian in it, with fresh salads, open sandwiches, and daily specials of pasta, but it also offers a sushi bar for those wanting to mix it up a little.

A tiny little place with a few benches seating just about two people at a time, **Gusto Deli Café** (corner of Five Ways, Broughton St., Paddington, tel. 02/9361-5640, daily

7am-7pm, croissant $3, sandwich $11) is frequented by people snuggled in the corner with a book or a newspaper, taking their time over coffee. A great selection of sandwiches and not-run-of-the-mill salads (think quinoa and beetroot) are all on tempting display, and you simply cannot have a coffee without accompanying it with a fresh *pain au chocolat*. This is the perfect place to rest your weary feet after traipsing through picture-perfect Paddington.

★ **Four in Hand** (105 Sutherland St., tel. 02/9326-1999, www.fourinhand.com.au, Tues.-Sun. noon-2:30pm and 6pm-late, bar mains $24) is a gastro pub hidden away in the residential streets of Paddington, and a gem at that. It's not cheap, but the atmosphere and the food make up for that. While there is fine dining in the main restaurant, try the bar instead—the setting is more relaxed, decorated in black and white with chrome bar stools around the finely tiled floors of the bar hub, and solid wooden tables and chairs make it classy and cozy at the same time. The bar menu gives you a good idea of the type of food Four in Hand offers, with salt cod and chorizo croquettes, and more offbeat items such as pig's-ear schnitzel. The beef burger with beetroot is excellent.

Rather than going to the Italian restaurant **10 William Street** (10 William St., Paddington, tel. 02/9360-3310, weekdays 5pm-late, Fri.-Sat. noon-midnight, no reservations, share plates and light lunch from $14, dinner mains $42) for dinner, which is delicious but can be pricey, try a late breakfast/early lunch on Friday or Saturday, which will give you a perfect excuse to have the English muffin with egg and sausage, listed under antipasti. The atmosphere is bustling, very much French café, lending itself to a lazy lunch, with the menu on the blackboard and different sized tables to linger at.

A sister restaurant to celebrity chef Matt Moran's Aria Restaurant, **Chiswick Restaurant** (65 Ocean St., Woollahra, tel. 02/8388-8688, www.chiswickrestaurant.com.au, Mon.-Thurs. noon-2:30pm and 6pm-10pm, Fri.-Sat. noon-3pm and 5:30pm-10pm, Sun. noon-3pm and 6pm-9:30pm, mains $30) is more relaxed and affordable, and the food is still fantastic. The large windows and French doors allow views to the garden behind the restaurant while watching the chefs, maybe even *the* chef, do their thing inside in the open kitchen. The fresh, seasonal modern Australian cuisine is locally sourced, often from the chef's own farm. Try the fish and prawn pie, or the wood-roasted lamb (from the chef's farm) to share.

THE NORTHERN SHORE

If you are looking for great views, you'll find them at **The Deck** (1 Olympic Dr., Milsons Point, tel. 02/9033-7670, www.thedecksydney.com.au, bar Wed.-Thurs. 11am-11pm, Fri.-Sat. 11am-late, Sun. 11am-9pm; restaurant Wed.-Sun. noon-8pm). By Luna Park, looking through the bridge at the opera house, with ferries bustling past, this is a great setting. With Luna Park in the background, it is not necessarily a quiet setting for a romantic dinner, but it's perfect for drinks and a plate of food to share: The confit rabbit pappardelle ($26) is great, and there is a children's menu. The menu offers an eclectic mix of world cuisine with, for example, Moroccan salad, Turkish fritters, paella, bouillabaisse, and Australian steak. Something for everybody.

In the lovely Art Deco swimming pools above the Olympic-length lanes, and nearly under the bridge, with views across the harbor, **Aqua Dining** (North Sydney Olympic Pool, corner Paul St. and Northcliff St., Milsons Point, tel. 02/9964-9998, www.aquadining.com.au, daily noon-9pm) has an unusual but great setting. The fine dining restaurant also has lounges outside, where you can enjoy a pre-dinner drink before indulging in this fine Italian menu and the very extensive wine list. The menu offers typical Italian fare brought up to an elegant fine-dining level, with an Australian twist, such as the emu fillet with broccolini and truffled honey ($39). Try to be on the outside veranda around sunset—it's quite magical.

Epi d'Or (Shop 11, Bligh St., North Sydney,

tel. 02/9922-5613, Tues.-Sat. 7:30am-5pm, Sun. 7:30am-2pm) is a tiny little café bursting with French charm, wicker chairs, walls full of picture frames, and some of the best fresh bread and croissants in town. Bring a paper or a book and linger over coffee and pastries.

Named after the botanist Gerard Fothergill, who once occupied the building, ★ **The Botanist** (17 Willoughby St., Kirribilli, tel. 02/9954-4057, http://thebotanist.com.au, Wed.-Sun. 11am-midnight, Mon. and Tues. 4pm-11pm) is botanically inspired in its decor, mix of cocktails, and fresh seasonal food ingredients. It's famous for its sliders, a cross between a mini-burger and a sandwich, which come in several varieties, such as pulled pork and crab—perfect for sharing or as light snacks ($20 for four pieces). There are other sharing options, such as grilled haloumi with pomegranate, lamb skewers, or braised beef cheeks with polenta. They also do great brunch every weekend.

★ **The Bathers' Pavilion** (4 The Esplanade, Balmoral, tel. 02/9969-5050, www.batherspavilion.com.au, café daily 7am-10pm, breakfast $18, lunch $20, dinner $22; restaurant daily noon-3pm and 6pm-10pm, mains $50, degustation menu $145) is a stunning old pavilion overlooking the lovely Balmoral Beach, in a little cove just along from Mosman and Taronga Zoo. The building has been divided into a relaxed café and a more fine-dining restaurant, both absolutely lovely. The café is accented with stylish colorful napkins and cushions, reflecting the sunny attitude of the whole place. This is the perfect place to relax over a lazy brunch on the weekend, maybe before or after taking a dip off the beach or walking in the parkland. The Big Balmoral Breakfast, served in the café, complete with eggs, toast, mushrooms, and hash browns, will set you back $25, but it will last all day.

THE BEACHES

★ **El Topo** (Level 3, The Eastern Hotel, Bondi Junction, www.eltopo.com.au, Mon. 6pm-10pm, Tues.-Sun. noon-3pm and 6pm-10pm, mains $15) is not your average Tex-Mex restaurant, but a Mexican restaurant specializing in the cuisine of the Oaxaca region. El Topo not only sourced all its colorful typical-for-the-region interior decor, complete with grinning skulls, bright tiles, and dancing skeletons, in the Oaxaca region, but it also serves a mean taco and well-aged vintage tequila, recommended by the in-house tequila and mescal "sommelier." On the "share with friends" menu you'll find fried crickets, which incidentally taste nutty with a hint of lime. The best dishes include the charred corn side dishes and the mushroom quesadilla, followed by the coconut flan, but you could also easily go with the kingfish ceviche, which is feather-light, and the spicy chorizo with slow-cooked egg and turtle beans. The atmosphere is part of the deal—colorful, busy, festive—so grab some friends and plan to spend a long evening.

Recently voted one of the best pizzerias in Sydney, **Pompei's** (126-130 Roscoe St., Bondi, tel. 02/9365-1233, www.pompeis.com.au, Fri.-Sun. 11:30am-11pm, Tues.-Thurs. 4:30pm-11pm, pizza $24) not only makes great pizza, but also their own gelato—a prize-winning combination just a stone's throw from the beach, complete with beach atmosphere—open, modern, and relaxed. Try the popular *speck e funghi trifolati* pizza with smoked prosciutto and a variety of wild mushrooms.

At ★ **Three Blue Ducks** (143 Macpherson St., Bronte, tel. 02/9389-0010, www.threeblueducks.com, daily 7:30am-11:30am and noon-2:30pm, Wed.-Sat. 6pm-11pm), a lovely small restaurant café where you can sit and people-watch, enjoying the simple but delicious food, which has recently been immortalized in a cookbook by the young owners. Try the famous steak sandwich ($10), the beetroot and haloumi salad with spiced pistachio praline ($21), or steamed mussels with herb, coconut sambal, and chili toast ($28), all served in easy comfortable surroundings.

Located by the park next to the beach, the **Bogey Hole Café** (473 Bronte Rd., Bronte, tel. 02/9389-8829, www.bogeyholecafe.com, daily 7am-4pm and 5:30pm-8:30pm) is perfect for lunch after a dip in the sea, which is very apt, as the café was named for a local rock pool (*bogey* in the local Aboriginal language denotes a place that is safe for swimming). The food is simple and healthy—try the cauliflower, quinoa, and chickpea salad ($17), or indulge in the all-day breakfast. Daily specials can be found on the large blackboard.

If you like seafood, ★ **Garfish** (1/39 East Esplanade, Manly, tel. 02/9977-0707, www.garfish.com.au, daily noon-3pm and 5:30pm-10pm) is the best place to come to. The decor is simple and stylish, with a large blackboard over the open kitchen and large windows allowing views across the water and the bustling ferry wharf. The menu is brimming with local and international fish. The signature dish is a snapper pie ($34), which is simply gorgeous. But there are also grilled options, catch of the day, and a couple of choices for meat-eaters, plus fresh oysters. And for dessert try the Belgian waffles. Overlooking Manly Bay, this is a definite favorite, if you are into fish.

Information and Services

TOURIST INFORMATION

There are two main branches of the **Sydney Visitor Centre,** one in The Rocks (corner Playfair St. and Argyle St., tel. 02/8273-0000, www.therocks.com.au, daily 9:30am-5:30pm) and another at Darling Harbour (33 Wheat St., behind Starbucks and IMAX Cinema, tel. 02/9211-4288, www.darlingharbour.com, daily 9:30am-5:30pm), with three additional kiosks: outside the Town Hall (George St.), at Circular Quay (corner Pitt St. and Albert St.), and in Haymarket (Dixon St. near Goulburn St.).

HOSPITALS, EMERGENCY SERVICES, AND PHARMACIES

Sydney has some of the country's best hospitals within its city limits. **Sydney Hospital** (6 Macquarie St., CBD, tel. 02/9382-7111), **Royal North Shore** (Pacific Highway, St. Leonards, tel. 02/9926-7111), and **St. Vincent's Hospital** (390 Victoria St., Darlinghurst, tel. 02/8382-1111), as well as the country's best children's hospital, **Sydney Children's Hospital** (High St., Randwick, tel. 02/9382-1111), are all equipped for around-the-clock emergencies.

There are countless pharmacies in the city, such as **CBD Pharmacy** (92 Pitt St., CBD, tel. 02/9221-0091, daily 7:45am-6:30pm). Some have extended hours, such as **Bondi Day and Night Pharmacy** (132 Campbell Parade, Bondi Beach, tel. 02/9130-4566, daily 8am-10pm) or **PriceLine Pharmacy** (Ground Level 9, World Square Retail, 644 George St., CBD, tel. 02/9268-0042, Mon.-Fri. 8:30am-10pm, Sat. 10am-8pm, Sun. 11am-6pm).

MONEY

There are branches of most larger banks throughout the inner city, on most main streets and shopping centers. Banks are generally open Monday to Friday from 9:30am to 4:30pm or 5pm depending on the bank. There are automated teller machines (ATMs) in and outside most branches, in malls, around travel hubs such as train stations, and even in some pubs and convenience stores. Most ATMs accept major international credit cards, which are also accepted in all major shops, cafés, and restaurants, except for maybe at market stalls. Foreign money exchange kiosks can be found along George Street, Circular Quay, and all major tourist areas.

Main bank branches are **HSBC** (570 George St., Town Hall, CBD, tel. 02/8113-2753), **Westpac** (283-285 Kent St., CBD, tel. 02/8254-2750), and **Citibank** (2 Park St., Ground Floor, Citigroup Centre, CBD, tel. 02/8225-1860).

POSTAL SERVICES

The **Sydney GPO Shop** is at 1 Martin Place in the CBD (tel. 13/13-18, Mon.-Fri. 8:15am-5:30pm, Sat. 10am-2pm), and there's another at 264a George Street, CBD (tel. 13/13-18, Mon.-Fri. 8:30am-5:30pm). Most newsagents and many postcard sellers also sell stamps.

INTERNET AND TELEPHONE

If you have a laptop or a smartphone, you can get free Wi-Fi connections at the following locations: Customs House, Town Hall, Ultimo, Haymarket, Kings Cross, and many cafés and restaurants in the city. The public libraries throughout the city also provide computers and Internet access for a nominal fee, and around the TAFE (Technical and Further Education) colleges in Ultimo, Haymarket, there are plenty of printing places that allow you to print from the Internet or a USB drive for a few cents per page.

Cell phones' compatibility with U.S. phones can be a problem, but even if yours is working abroad, the costs of international roaming can easily spiral out of control. If you feel you will absolutely need a cell phone, stop off at the Optus shop in the airport, or any mobile phone shop in the city, and get yourself a local SIM card or an Australian starter kit. Telstra, Optus, and Vodafone all have prepaid mobile systems that are easily available and quick to set up. The kits start from around $30. Alternatively, there are still public call boxes in the city, taking coins and international calling cards.

Getting Around

Trains, light rail, buses, ferries—Sydney has it all. The public transport system is so extensive and reliable that it makes a car pretty much unnecessary, and you can generally save yourself a taxi fare.

GETTING TO AND FROM THE AIRPORT

Sydney's **Kingsford Smith Airport** (SYD, Airport Dr., tel. 02/9667-9111, www.sydneyairport.com.au), named after a local pioneer in flying but often and confusingly called Mascot Airport, is roughly a 20-minute taxi ride ($30), airport express train (every 6-7 minutes, $17.20 one way), or bus ride (Sydney Airporter, www.kst.com.au, online pre-booking service to and from the airport, regular departures, adult $15, child $10 each way) from your hotel. Unless you are traveling on your own, a taxi works out cheapest and probably is most convenient. The train is fast and easy but won't drop you off right by your hotel. Because the airport is on the south border of Sydney's sprawl and the runway extends into Botany Bay, the approach over Sydney is one of the most beautiful in the world, giving you views over the harbor, the opera house, and the bridge—if you are in the right seat and the weather is in your favor, of course.

Security is pretty much the same as everywhere in the world upon departure, though upon arrival, the checks are intense due to Australia's strict import laws. No food, plant, or animal items, dead or alive, not even an apple left over from the journey, are allowed into the country, and getting caught inadvertently "smuggling" something in can lead to serious delays and inconvenience after a long flight. Make sure there is nothing in your checked luggage, and double-check your hand luggage before leaving the plane.

Three terminals, including international (T1), domestic (T2), and domestic Qantas only (T3), serve Sydney well, and the airport is spacious and comfortable and has plenty of shops and cafés to while away any waiting time.

PUBLIC TRANSPORT

The main hubs are the Central Railway Station to the south of CBD, and Circular

Quay to the north. From either of those you can connect to anywhere in the CBD and surrounding suburbs, with buses having the widest reach into the depth of the suburbs. The train system is extensive and is best for quick connections between north and south of the harbor, or from the CBD west and east, but the reach is not as comprehensive as those of the buses. For timetable and connection information access www.sydneytrains.info.

The Sydney buses run nearly 24 hours a day, charging from $2.20 to $4.60 for a single adult fare, depending on distance traveled. Trains and ferries start from around 5am or 6am and run until past midnight. The Sydney Trains and NSW TrainLink networks run hand-in-hand (fares from $3.60 for rides of less than 10 km, increasing with distance to $8.40 for a single adult fare). Ferry fares run $5.80 to $7.20 for a single adult fare depending on distance traveled. Most local commuters use a mix of public transport options (such as ferry and bus or train and bus) to reach their destination, and even the ticketing options are set up for individual options. The same goes for travelers, although access to most major sights is quite streamlined and easy.

The **MyMulti tickets** issued from **Transport for NSW** (www.transport.nsw.gov.au, tel. 13/15-00) encompass travel by train, bus, ferry, and light rail, and an adult one-day ticket costs up to $24, including all zones and modes of transport. Notable exceptions are some private ferry companies, which run a handful of express ferries. The MyZone fare system allows you to choose tickets that are just bus, train, or ferry or more than one mode of transport. Selecting which zones you will travel within and which mode of transport you will use will give you the best and cheapest option. These tickets come in passes lasting from one single trip to one-day, weekly, monthly, quarterly, or annual passes, with student and pensioner (senior) discounts available, too. If you are in Sydney for any longer than two days, the weekly MyMulti ticket for $46 covers all eventualities, and you can hop onto buses, trains, and ferries within Zone 1, which is pretty much all of Sydney, as many times as you need to.

On Sundays you can purchase a Family Funday Ticket at $2.50 per person as long as the traveling group includes one child and one adult. These tickets allow you to go anywhere in Sydney, on the entire Sydney Trains and NSW TrainLink networks, plus all government ferries and buses. This means you could go all the way up to Newcastle or to the Blue Mountains for $2.50 each.

To find your way around the city's extensive public transport options, load the **NSW Transport Info** app onto your smartphone. This app allows you to put in your current location and your destination, giving you details of all the modes of transport available to get you there. It even gives you directions if there is some walking involved. Alternatively, log on to www.transportnsw.info, the NSW Transport Info website, which gives you all the information you will need to find the best way to your destination.

TAXIS

Taxis are all regulated and metered, and can be hailed at taxi ranks, off the street, and by telephone. Some of the most popular taxi companies are **ABC Cabs** (tel. 13/25-22), **Manly Cabs** (tel. 13/16-68), **Premier Cabs** (tel. 13/10-17), **Silver Service** (tel. 13/31-00), and **Taxis Combined** (tel. 13/33-00). For a rough estimate of taxi fares across the city, try www.taxifare.com.au; if you have your set-off point and destination, it will give you an estimate.

Aussie Water Taxis (tel. 02/9211-7730, www.aussiewatertaxis.com) can be booked by phone or online and take you wherever you want to go in Sydney Harbour. One-way trips from Darling Harbour to Taronga Zoo, for example, would cost you $25 per adult and $15 per child, with a round-trip usually saving you $5.

DRIVING

If you intend to drive, Sydney's roads are safe, comfortable, and get you where you want to go without too much scope for getting lost. Commuter traffic is, like in all cities around the world, a major pain, with delays exactly where you don't want them. Here as everywhere in the world, try to avoid the roads 7am-9:30am and 5pm-6:30pm. So, if you have a choice, opt for public transport to get around.

Sydney has some easy connections with major highways reaching out into the various suburbs: The Pacific Highway connects the CBD across Sydney Harbour Bridge with the north, indeed all the way to Brisbane and beyond. There is a toll fare charged when crossing Sydney Harbour Bridge southbound only, and the same system works for the Sydney Harbour Tunnel, with tolls charged at $4 each time. Once on the north side, Military Road gets you to most suburbs along the way to Manly.

Southbound, the Southern Cross Drive connects easiest to the airport, while Parramatta Road is a fast westward commute to Parramatta past the docks and Sydney Olympic Park. Toward the east, Oxford Street winds itself through the suburbs; it's not fast, but it hits all the main suburbs along the way to Bondi Beach and is the route of choice for the buses, too.

Once you are heading out of the sprawling city limits, you may well encounter further toll roads, including the Eastern Distributor, which is only charged northbound; the M5 East Freeway and the M5 South-West Motorway, both charged in each direction; the Westlink M7, the Hills M2 Motorway, and both the Lane Cove and the Cross City tunnels, which are all charged in each direction.

Parking is a continuous bugbear with all Sydneysiders, as it is limited and expensive. Rates vary with location and peak hours, but in the CBD parking meter tariffs are $7 per hour weekdays 8am-6pm and $3 per hour on weekends. Secure parking can be even more pricey.

Blue Mountains

Some 50 kilometers west of Sydney, the Blue Mountains are a range of geological sandstone plateaus, escarpments, and gorges, covering an area of some 10,300 square kilometers, around 1,150 meters high. Originally named by Governor Arthur Phillip in 1788 as the Carmarthen Hills (for the northern section near Sydney) and the Lansdowne Hills (for the southern), the Blue Mountains soon got their current name due to the blue color the mountains seem to shimmer in due to the haze of eucalyptus oils from the more than 90 different species of eucalyptus tree found in the region.

Although officially called the Blue Mountains, the region really is all about the valleys and gorges, not the mountains. You will not see a rugged mountainscape as you approach, but rather find the beauty when climbing down from the plateaus into the eroded gorges of up to 760 meters depth.

Added to the UNESCO World Heritage list in 2000 because of their diversity and geological uniqueness, the Blue Mountains cover seven national parks and a conservation reserve. The main center is **Katoomba,** a bustling town on the edge of the Jamison Valley, from where most tours, attractions, and hikes start.

SIGHTS
Blue Mountains Cultural Centre

Opened in November 2012, the **Blue Mountains Cultural Centre** (30 Parke St., Katoomba, tel. 02/4780-5410, www.bluemountainsculturalcentre.com.au, Mon.-Fri. 10am-5pm, Sat.-Sun. 10am-2pm, adult $5, child under 18 free) features the Blue Mountains City Art Gallery, showcasing local artists, and the World Heritage Exhibition, devoted to education about the distinctive

Blue Mountains

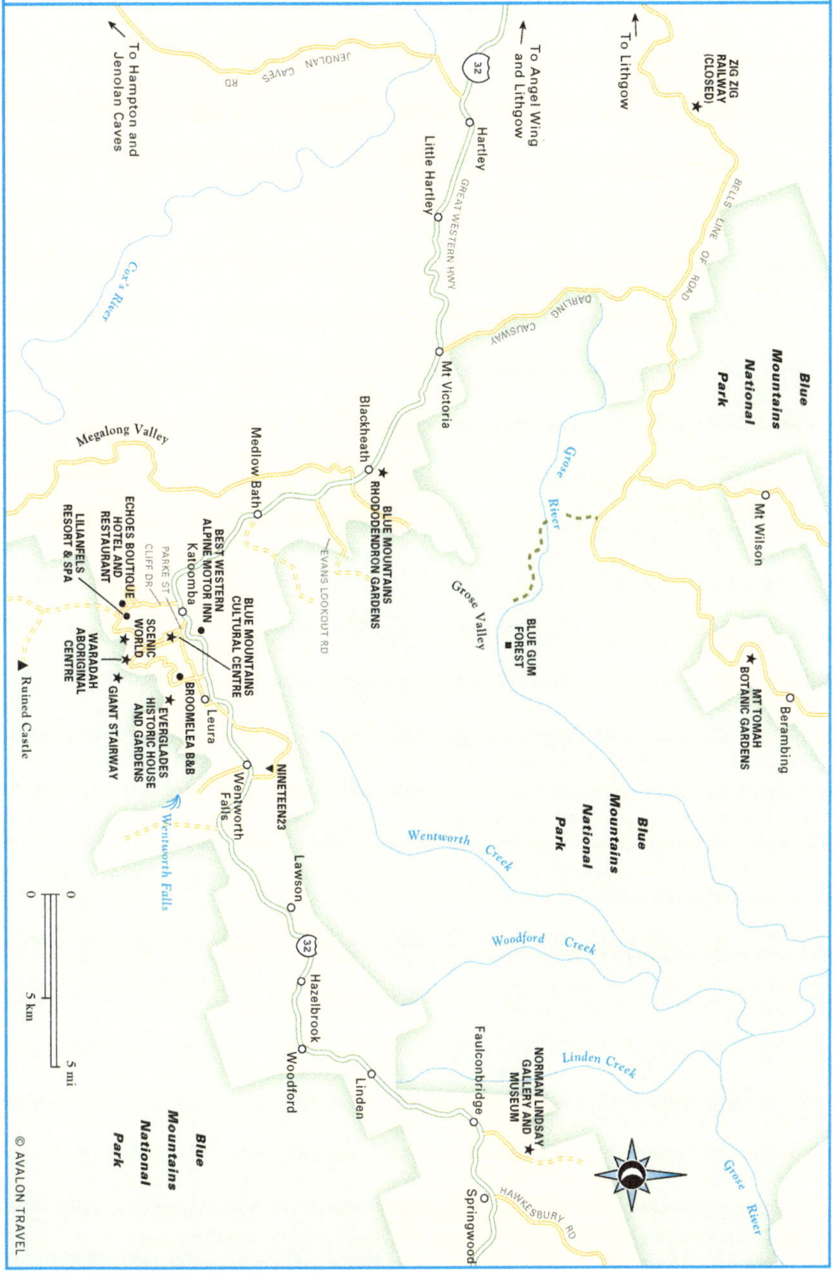

environment, history, and culture of the Blue Mountains region. The Cultural Centre also houses the new Katoomba Library and showcases innovative, diverse, distinctive, and creative cultural programs. And the gift shop is one of the best around.

Scenic World

Scenic World (1 Violet St., Katoomba, tel. 02/4780-0200, www.scenicworld.com.au, daily 9am-5pm, adult $35, child 4-13 $18, family $88) is a fantastic mix of fun rides and nature. There is a large center at the top of the Jamison Valley, and from there you have three ride options: First is the **Katoomba Scenic Railway,** the steepest railway in the world according to the *Guinness Book of Records,* descending at an angle of 52 degrees; it was originally part of the Katoomba mining tramways constructed between 1878 and 1900. Second is the **Scenic Skyway,** a glass-bottom aerial cable car that traverses an arm of the Jamison Valley at Katoomba and offers stunning views across to the various rock formations, including the Three Sisters, Orphan Rock, and the lovely Katoomba Waterfalls. Third is the **Scenic Flyway,** another record-breaking ride—this time it's the steepest aerial cable car in Australia, showcasing the valley below.

The best way to get the most out of the rides and the scenery is to go down the valley either by the Scenic Flyway or the train, then enjoy either a short bushwalk or longer option in the valley below (there are maps along the way giving you details of directions and approximate timing; the longest walk takes less than one hour), and then go up again by the option other than the descent one. Do it all again in reverse. Then take the Skyway across to the lookout platform, take pictures, and ride back. The tickets allow you to take as many rides as you wish, and with each ride only taking a few minutes, you can have endless fun and get the most out of the stunning valley setting. Estimate at least two hours for this stop.

Katoomba Scenic Railway in Scenic World

Waradah Aboriginal Centre

A proud celebration of Aboriginal culture, art, and dance, **Waradah Aboriginal Centre** (World Heritage Plaza, Echo Point, Katoomba, tel. 02/4782-1979, www.waradah.com.au, daily 9am-5pm, adult $10, child $5) is a landmark product, showcasing the extraordinary talents of local artists. Next to the viewing platforms at Echo Point, the brief (30-minute) performance, every 30 minutes on the hour and half hour, is an ideal way to experience authentic song and dance performances and Dreamtime stories as told by the local peoples. Watch the energetic corroboree (dance) and didgeridoo performances performed in costume and traditional paint. A gallery next door showcases some lovely Aboriginal art.

Jenolan Caves

Just an hour from Katoomba and a 2.5-hour drive from Sydney, the **Jenolan Caves** (4655 Jenolan Caves Rd., Jenolan Caves, tel. 1300/763-311, www.jenolancaves.org.au) are the world's oldest cave system, and with some

10 different caves to explore, they're some of the world's most spectacular, too. Legend has it that it was an outlaw who was hiding from his potential prosecutors who happened upon the first cave, only to get deeper and deeper, uncovering a truly magical underground system that stuns with its 340-million-year-old history.

There are tours for all fitness and adventure levels available. The basic option ($32 adult, $22 child, and $75 for families) allows you to choose Chifley Cave, Imperial Cave, or Lucas Cave, and tours range 60-90 minutes. There are many additional caves, and tour prices vary.

One of the most stunning caves is probably **Lucas Cave,** which contains one of Jenolan's highest and largest chambers. The internal chambers are connected with some 910 steps, at times very steep but manageable, giving it a level three difficulty rating. **Imperial Cave,** a level one cave with 258 steps, follows an underwater river passage. **Chifley Cave,** with its examples of special spar crystal, is a level two with 421 steps.

If you're after more excitement, try one of the **Adventure Caving** tours, where you can go properly caving, suited up in coveralls, helmets, and ropes, needing to squeeze through tight spaces, rappel, and challenge yourself in the dark. The "Plughole Adventure" does not require previous experience and takes approximately two hours ($90 pp, minimum age 10, all equipment provided). The slightly more advanced "Aladdin Cave Adventure" takes three hours (all equipment provided, $100 pp, minimum age 12).

There are, in addition to the caves, many other reasons to spend time at Jenolan Caves. Many self-guided nature trails of various lengths meander through the caves' beautiful surroundings, including a walk to **Blue Lake,** which is a habitat of the shy platypus. The historic **Caves House** (tel. 1300/763-311, www.jenolancaves.org.au, from $135), a hotel on the heritage register, is right next to the caves' entrance. It's a perfect place to spend a night, giving you more time to explore.

Everglades Historic House and Gardens

At **Everglades Historic House and Gardens** (37 Everglades Ave., Leura, tel. 02/4784-1938, www.everglades.org.au, fall and winter daily 10am-4pm, spring and summer daily 10am-5pm, adult $10, child $4), a beautiful heritage garden is set around a historic home from the 1930s. But here you

the fantastic formations inside the Jenolan Caves

get not only the lovely gardens, flowers, and sculpted hedges, but also stunning views across Jamison Valley and the surrounding area. Features include various follies and water features, a gift shop, and tea rooms, and depending on when you are visiting, there can be a riot of color of the seasonal flowers, with tulips and bluebells demanding attention at times. The house itself is well worth seeing, especially the Art Deco bathrooms.

The Zig Zag Railway

Unfortunately, this scenic and historic railway was completely destroyed in the November 2013 bushfires with no immediate plans of reopening.

RECREATION

The **Blue Mountains Adventure Company** (84a Bathurst Rd., Katoomba, tel. 02/4782-1271, www.bmac.com.au) offers rappelling, rock climbing, caving, and bushwalking to fully appreciate the challenges the mountains and gorges can throw at you. Even if you are a novice, you could challenge yourself and take part in a day's introductory rappelling, learning the skill and practicing at various terrains, working your way up to the final rappel down a 55-meter rock face ($195 pp).

Hiking is one of the best ways to see the Blue Mountains and its valleys. Try the **Giant Staircase Walk,** which kicks off at **Echo Point** lookout point and covers a distance of 3.5 kilometers. It takes roughly three hours one way. It does, as the name suggests, include a 900-step staircase, made from steel and with handrails. The really good news is that at the bottom, there is a scenic easy walk and a potential ride on the world's steepest railway back up the slope (run by Scenic World, adult $14, child $8)—although you could climb back up. For directions, check in the **Blue Mountains Visitor Information Centre** at Echo Point (Echo Point Rd., Katoomba, tel. 1300/653-408, www.bluemountainscitytourism.com.au). There are several other walks of varying length and difficulty; choose something that suits you at www.bluemts.com.au and find detailed maps at Echo Point.

Centennial Glen Stables (Kanimbla Dr. via Shipley Rd., Blackheath, tel. 02/4787-1193, www.centennialglenstables.com, from $110) offers **sulky driving**—basically driving a two-wheel horse carriage across a farm track in the mountains. The sulky carries two people and the ride is a little more sedate than riding the horse itself. You can take a picnic and extend the one-hour ride, if you wish, to take in more of the scenery. You can also combine the sulky tour with horse riding, with two on the carriage and someone else alongside on the horse.

Trail ride and wine tasting tours are offered by **Adrenalin Tours** (www.adrenalin.com.au, tel. 1300/791-793, from $89). Visit the only winery in the Blue Mountains, the Dryridge Estate, and enjoy a cheese platter, some of the home-grown Cabernet Sauvignon or Riesling, and then head back on your horse. It's a lovely way to enjoy the surroundings, but make sure you don't overdo the drinking and riding.

ACCOMMODATIONS

Stay in a home called **Angel Wing** (Jenolan Caves Rd., www.contemporaryhotels.com.au/blue-mountains/angel, tel. 02/9331-2881, $1,100 per night, minimum stay two nights), perched high on a hill near the Jenolan Caves with stunning views across the valleys. The open-plan house is a treat in itself, with floor to ceiling windows, an open fire, contemporary furnishings, and superior linens and toiletries. It sleeps up to eight persons. Or try the **Echoes Boutique Hotel & Restaurant** (3 Lilianfels Ave., Katoomba, tel. 02/4782-1966, www.echoeshotel.com.au, from $319). Overlooking the Jamison Valley, Echoes is a small hotel that evolved from a B&B yet retained its personal touch, with some added luxuries, such as its fine-dining restaurant. The rooms are spacious and comfortable, with the suites offering sitting areas with amazing views, and the terrace of the restaurant must surely be one of the best places to enjoy vistas of the Blue Mountains.

The fabulous **Lilianfels Resort and Spa** (Lilianfels Ave., Katoomba, tel. 02/4780-1200, www.lilianfels.com.au, from $249) is a gorgeous old villa overlooking the valleys, with a traditional old-world atmosphere about it. You can just imagine tourists in the early 1900s staying here. Plush furniture, pretty curtains and wallpaper, and a chandelier in the restaurant all add to the charm. Perfectly located within a five-minute walk to the iconic Three Sisters rock formation and the town center, this is a lovely place to stay. On a smaller scale, try the **Broomelea Bed & Breakfast** (273, The Mall, Leura, tel. 02/4784-2940, www.broomelea.com.au, from $175), a rustic little bed-and-breakfast place offering rooms, suites, and one self-contained cottage. There are four-poster beds, roaring open log fires, and timber beams, making it a very cozy place to stay, especially if it's chilly outside.

If you are on a budget, you could do a lot worse than the **Best Western Alpine Motor Inn** (Great Western Highway, corner Camp St., Katoomba, tel. 02/4782-2011, www.alpine.bestwestern.com.au, from $143). It's a no-frills but clean and roomy motel accommodation in a central location, offering an easy family stay with the option of interconnecting rooms, within easy reach of all the Blue Mountains attractions. If you are out all day and just need a budget-friendly place to crash at night, this ticks the boxes.

FOOD

Step back in time to the early 1900s at the **Paragon Cafe and Restaurant** (65 Katoomba St., Katoomba, tel. 02/4782-2928, Sun.-Fri. 10am-4pm, Sat. 10am-10:30pm). This little café/restaurant offers a time capsule with decor, furniture, and even the music in the style of the 1920s, with diners sitting in little wood-fitted alcoves, enjoying the coffee and hand-made chocolates. Come for coffee and scones, a light lunch of toasted sandwiches ($13.50), or a large portion of fish and chips ($18.50). And do go and explore the two back rooms, one a stylish cocktail lounge, the other a private dining room. There is also a display of old cash registers.

Nineteen23 (1 Lake St., Wentworth Falls, tel. 04/8836-1923, www.nineteen23.com.au, Thurs.-Sun. 6pm-late, lunch Sat.-Sun. noon-late, five-course menu $55) is, as the name suggests, also set in a 1920s heritage building, and offers fine dining in beautiful surroundings. The head chef comes from having headed a celebrity restaurant back in Melbourne and offers a seasonal menu that changes regularly, literally keeping things fresh. If the weather plays ball, reserve a table on the veranda overlooking the mountains. It's stunning.

The **Leura Garage** (84 Railway Parade, Leura, tel. 02/4784-3391, www.leuragarage.com.au, Sat.-Thurs. 12:30pm-late, closed Fri.) is a rustic and bustling place where the food is served on wooden boards. Look around at the displays of interesting materials, covering anything from twigs to leather and stones, used for the decor as well as the art installations. The corn on the cob with smoked paprika butter ($14) and the sticky pork ribs ($24) are definite favorites.

Pop into **Sassafras Creek** (83 Old Bells Line of Road, Kurrajong, tel. 02/4573-0988, www.sassafrascreek.com.au, Tues.-Thurs. 9am-4pm, Fri.-Sun. 9am-5pm, Fri.-Sat. dinner from 6:30pm), a lovely mix of gallery, florist, and café, with great simple yet tasty options. Try the soup of the day with crusty bread ($15) or the tarragon chicken breast with pancetta salad ($23), and then check out the offerings in the gallery. It's a destination in itself.

INFORMATION AND SERVICES

The superb **Blue Mountains Visitor Information Centre at Echo Point** (Echo Point Rd., Katoomba, tel. 1300/653-408, www.bluemountainscitytourism.com.au, daily 9am-5pm) is where to get information on things to do and where to stay and book tours. The staff also have intimate knowledge of all the hikes in the region and can give you

A Drive to Canberra

A mere three-hour drive from Sydney is Australia's very underrated capital city, Canberra, which celebrated its centenary in 2013. The city is a perfect place to spend a day or two with the entire family, taking in the museums, shopping, and seeing where Australia is ruled from.

In 1913, Australia's capital was established amid the rolling countryside at supposedly the halfway point between the ferociously competitive cities of Sydney and Melbourne, who both wanted the glory for themselves. The alleged halfway point is actually 287 kilometers from Sydney and 676 kilometers from Melbourne, but that is only good if you're coming from Sydney.

Depart Sydney via the M5 tollway heading south, connecting to Hume Highway 31, and after you've spotted the gigantic merino sheep sculpture in Goulburn, one of Australia's iconic "Big Things," turn onto the Federal Highway to Canberra. It's easy and scenic all the way.

If you are there during the week, don't miss the open-to-the-public question time at 2pm weekdays at the **Parliament House** (Parliament Dr., tel. 02/6277-7111, www.aph.gov.au, open on non-sitting days 9am-5pm) dominating Canberra's many traffic circles. Question time tickets for the House of Representatives can be booked during office hours by telephoning the Serjeant-at-Arm's Office (tel. 02/6277-4889) up until 12:30pm on the day required.

Once you've seen where Australia's laws come from, go and see where its coins are made. The **Royal Australian Mint** (Denison St., Deakin, tel. 02/6202-6999, www.ramint.gov.au, Mon.-Fri. 8:30am-5pm, Sat.-Sun. 10am-4pm, free) produces every single coin in circulation in Australia and has a great exhibition of the evolution of money throughout the years.

If you have kids to keep happy, head straight for the **Questacon** at the **National Science and Technology Centre** (King Edward Terrace, Parkes, tel. 02/6270-2800, www.questacon.edu.au, daily 9am-5pm, adult $23, child $17.50, family with three children $70), where there are interactive exhibits such as the earthquake house, moving magma, caged lightning, and much more. Plan to be here at least a couple of hours.

Just around the corner lies the **National Gallery of Australia** (Parkes Place, Parkes, tel. 02/6240-6411, www.nga.gov.au, daily 10am-5pm, free, but fees for special exhibitions), holding more than 120,000 pieces of artwork and sculptures, including many pieces of Aboriginal and Torres Strait Islander art. The gallery is always holding special exhibitions, many of which are unique to Australia.

Just 35 kilometers southwest of Canberra lies the fascinating **Canberra Deep Space Communication Complex** (421 Discovery Dr., Paddys River, tel. 02/6201-7880, www.cdscc.nasa.gov, daily 9am-5pm, free), a ground station that is part of the Deep Space Network run by NASA's Jet Propulsion Laboratory and is one of just three in the world. You can see a real moon rock weighing in at 142 grams, which is the largest piece of moon rock outside the United States, and can track flight paths of manned missions and satellites that are currently ongoing.

Stay at **East Hotel** (69 Canberra Ave., tel. 02/6295-6925, www.east.com.au, from $180), a trendy aparthotel full of art and stylish quirkiness, with a great restaurant downstairs. Centrally located near the parliament, it is within walking distance of the swanky suburbs of Kingston and Manuka Village, both with great individual boutique shops and cafés. If you are in town on a Sunday, go to the **Old Bus Depot Markets** (21 Wentworth Ave., Kingston, tel. 02/6295-3331, Sun. 10am-4pm) which offer food stalls, handicrafts, jewelry, collectibles, and pretty much something for everybody.

---

detailed advice on where to go and how long it will take, sign you in and out, and provide detailed maps of each walk.

GETTING THERE AND AROUND

The easiest and most flexible way to travel the Blue Mountains is by car. The entrance to the Blue Mountains at Glenbrook/Lapstone is only around a 50-minute drive west from Sydney. From the city, take the A4 (City West Link) and follow the signs to Parramatta; the M4 Motorway starts at Strathfield and takes you through to Lapstone in the Blue Mountains. Signs to Katoomba and the various attractions are easily followed from there.

Alternatively, you can travel to Katoomba by rail: **Sydney Trains** (www.sydneytrains.info) and **NSW TrainLink** (www.nswtrainlink.info) offer an extremely efficient service to the Blue Mountains (from $11.40 off-peak). If you are flying into Sydney, you can connect directly from Sydney Airport to Central Railway Station by CityRail, or take one of the many shuttle buses. From Central Station, you can catch the air-conditioned double-decker Mountains train, which will get you into Katoomba within two hours. It leaves every hour. If you have a three-zone multi-day or weekly public transport pass (from $22 per day), you can use that without having to pay extra.

Several coach tours pick you up from your hotel in the morning, take you to the Blue Mountains, and include many attractions, such as the Jenolan Caves. Try **AAT Kings** (www.aatkings.com, Blue Mountains and Jenolan Caves $149), or **Life's an Adventure** (www.lifesanadventure.com.au, from $299 for personalized 4WD tour), which offers hiking and four-wheel-drive tours to the mountains. Generally, all these tours pick you up from your hotel early in the morning, around 7:30am, and deliver you straight back for dinnertime, although timing may vary slightly.

Once you are in Katoomba, there are a couple of easy ways to see what's on offer: **Blue Mountain Trolley Tours** (76 Main St., Katoomba, tel. 02/4782-7999, www.trolleytours.com.au, $25 per adult, $15 per child, $70 for a family) has 29 stops on a hop-on/hop-off basis covering the main region. The trolley bus departs hourly from Katoomba, and the company also offers packages that include entry tickets to Jenolan Caves and/or rides at Scenic World. The **Blue Mountains Explorer Bus** (Katoomba Railway Station, tel. 1300/300-915, www.explorerbus.com.au, adult $38, child $19, family $95) also follows the hop-on/hop-off system along the 29 stops across the Blue Mountains and offers live commentary. The bus departs every 30 minutes in the mornings and afternoons, with an hour's lunch break between 12:35pm and 1:35pm.

Hunter Valley

The Hunter Valley is Australia's oldest and New South Wales's largest wine-growing region. The first vines were planted around 1830 on the fertile flats of the undulating Hunter River and its many tributaries, and some 150 wineries produce over 39 million liters of premium wine annually, with favored grape varieties including Semillon, Chardonnay, Shiraz, and Cabernet Sauvignon. Since the first road was cut between Sydney and Newcastle, reaching inland to Willombi back in 1826, the region has expanded to cover 6,000 hectares of vineyards and has become a major weekend destination, with some 2.8 million annual visitors from Sydney and afar. The visitors are drawn not only by the fine wines, but also by the many resultant attractions that have sprung up around the wineries, offering anything from ballooning to spectacular gardens, from afternoon tea to fine dining, from carriage rides to cycling across the imposing Brokenback Range.

If you are driving (the best way to experience this part of NSW), the acknowledged hub for basing yourself is the tiny "village" of **Pokolbin,** with most attractions and events in the vicinity. Village may be the incorrect term to use, as both Pokolbin and Hunter Valley villages are a mere assortment of shops and amenities. **Hunter Valley Village** can be found within the locale of Hunter Valley Gardens and offers all the necessities of a village: a pharmacy and a general store together with numerous shops selling pretty knickknacks, pieces of arts and crafts, chocolates, wine, and many handsome souvenirs, plus a

Hunter Valley

generous assortment of restaurants and cafés. It's a perfect village, inviting visitors to leisurely stroll through it before exploring the gardens and tasting some wine.

The Hunter Valley is synonymous with festivals. There is always something going on in the Hunter Valley, with a fine array of events spread throughout the year. From operatic festivals to pop, there is something for every interest, something every month. Check www.winecountry.com.au before you set off.

WINERIES

With so many wineries, from large and established for generations to quirky, boutique, and relatively new, it is impossible to choose which ones to recommend, as wine is such a personal thing. However, some vineyards keep cropping up in conversation, keep winning awards, and are on the lips of most people in the know. Here is a selection.

In the business since 1866, the **Audrey Wilkinson Winery** (Debeyers Rd., Pokolbin, tel. 02/4998-7411, www.audreywilkinson.com.au, daily 10am-5pm) is widely regarded as the first wine vineyard in the Pokolbin area. Known for its Semillon, Verdelho, Gewürztraminer, Chardonnay, Shiraz, Merlot, Malbec, Tempranillo, Cabernet, and Muscat, and boasting spectacular views across the Hunter Valley, the vineyard was rated by *Gourmet Traveller Wine* as one of the "Top 10 Cellar Doors" in the country, and the only one in NSW.

Founded only some 40 years ago, **Brokenwood** (401-427 McDonalds Rd., Pokolbin, tel. 02/4998-7559, www.

brokenwood.com.au, daily 9:30am-5pm) has grapes that are consistently praised and have produced an award-winning Shiraz.

At **Constable Estate** (205 Gillards Rd., Pokolbin, tel. 02/4998-7887, www.constablevineyards.com.au, daily 10am-4pm) the draws, apart from the wine (Cabernet Sauvignon, Verdelho, Semillon, Shiraz, and Chardonnay), are the beautiful rose and camellia gardens, the sculpture park, and the various walks across the large estate. A small boutique estate with only 3,000 cases produced each year, it is, however, one of the most entertaining and pretty.

The immense tasting room at **Hope Estate** (2213 Broke Rd., Pokolbin, tel. 02/4998-7363, www.hopeestate.com.au, daily 10am-5pm), with 59 huge wooden casks (each holding 4,500 liters) and beamed ceilings, looks like an opera set and is popular as a wedding venue. Outside, there always seems to be a mob of kangaroos lazing on the lawn. Hope specializes in Verdelho, Semillon, Chardonnay, Shiraz, and Merlot.

Lindeman's (119 McDonalds Rd., Pokolbin, tel. 02/4998-7684, www.lindemans.com, daily 10am-5pm) is one of the oldest continuous Australian wineries, famous especially for its Shiraz, having been founded in 1843 by Dr Henry Lindeman with his wife Eliza at their property, Cawarra, in the Hunter Valley. Apart from the wine, a new drawing card to the vineyard is the 1843 Harvest Café, which offers seating inside and outdoors overlooking the valley.

In the Mount View area of the valley, **Pepper Tree** (Abbotsbury, Pokolbin, tel. 02/4909-7100, http://peppertreewines.com.au, daily 9am-5pm), winner of the Hunter Valley 2011 Cellar Door of the Year, is a benchmark for quality. Set among pristine gardens, a short walk from a historic convent building, Pepper Tree's vast vineyards are perfect for both sight and palate. Apart from its Chardonnay, Verdelho, Semillon, Shiraz, Viognier, Sauvignon Blanc, Merlot, Cabernet, Grenache, and Pinot Noir, the estate has also branched out into coffee blends.

Rosemount Estate (Rosemount Rd., Denman, tel. 02/6549-6400, www.rosemountestates.com, Mon.-Sat. 10am-5pm, Sun. 11am-5pm) was established by Robert Oatley and family in the Upper Hunter Valley in 1969. By 1976, Rosemount wines had won gold medals in Paris, Montpellier, Calcutta, and America, and today it's one of Australia's leading wine companies, with the Rosemount Estate Balmoral Syrah as the brand's flagship wine. They produce a wide range of wine, with something to suit both sophisticated tastes and everyday drinkers.

Tempus Two (corner Broke Rd. and McDonalds Rd., Pokolbin, tel. 02/4993-3999, www.tempustwo.com.au, daily 10am-5pm) is a boutique winery with a spaceship-like tasting room. The architect-designed cellar door features a Japanese restaurant with a sizzling teppanyaki grill and a trendy bar where you can learn to pour the perfect cocktail. The winery specializes in blending a distinctive range of wines from Australia's premier wine-growing regions.

Family-owned since 1858, and now headed up by fourth-generation family member Bruce Tyrrell, **Tyrrell's Wines** (1838 Broke Rd., Pokolbin, tel. 02/4993-7000, www.tyrrells.com.au, Mon.-Sat. 9am-5pm, Sun. 10am-4pm) is home to some of Australia's most acclaimed wines, including the iconic Vat 1 Semillon. Since 1971, Tyrrell's has been awarded over 5,000 trophies and medals and in 2010 was named "Winery of the Year" in James Halliday's *Australian Wine Companion*.

RECREATION

Barrington Tops National Park (Chichester, tel. 02/6538-5300, daily 24 hours, except in severe weather and fire events, free) is a rainforest reserve carved out of volcanic flows and is ideal for bushwalks, picnics, and fishing. The **Barrington Outdoor Adventure Centre** (www.boac.com.au, tel. 02/6558-2093, daily 9am-5pm) offers a range of exciting white-water kayaking, canoeing, and downhill mountain-biking adventures.

Hunter Valley Carriages (917 Hermitage

Rd., Pokolbin, tel. 04/3133-7367, www.huntervalleycarriages.com.au) offers horse riding ($45 for 30 minutes), pony rides (from $20), and two-hour trail rides ($55 pp). It also offers carriage rides ($160 pp, minimum three people) through the valley, taking in several wineries and lunch along the way—a great way to experience the beauty of the valley.

If you want to tour the region under your own steam, why not have a bike delivered right to your door? With **Hunter Valley Cycling** (tel. 04/1828-1480, www.huntervalleycycling.com.au, mountain bike $35/day, children's bike $20/day), you get all the gear, including bike, helmet, and maps, delivered to your accommodations.

Set on 25 hectares, **Hunter Valley Gardens** (2090 Broke Rd., tel. 02/4998-4000, www.huntervalleygardens.com.au, daily 9am-5pm, adult $26, child $15, family $57) has 12 themed gardens and eight kilometers of paths, making this a haven for garden lovers. Choose favorites such as the Rose Garden or Chinese Moongate Garden, or try the unique Indian Mosaic Garden, the enchanting Storybook Garden, or the Formal Garden. Or see them all, if you have enough time.

Hunter Valley Zoo (138 Lomas Ln., Nulkaba, tel. 02/4990-7714, www.huntervalleyzoo.com.au, Thurs.-Tues. 9am-4pm, adult $19, child $11, family $55) is a small zoo, but it has all the iconic Australian animals in residence. You can get close to a koala, nuzzle a kangaroo, pat a wombat, and stroke a reptile. There are dingoes, crocodiles, and Tasmanian devils, all on a manageable scale.

The Golden Door Health Retreat—Elysia (Thompsons Rd., Pokolbin, tel. 02/4993-8500, www.goldendoor.com.au) is a beautiful spa that overlooks the mountains and valleys, offering massages, facials, and more unique experiences, such as the watsu treatment, moor mud baths, and steam infusions.

Wine Country Ballooning (332 Lovedale Rd., Lovedale, tel. 02/4991-7533, from $239) gives you a whole new perspective of the lovely countryside. Glide over wineries and mountains, and maybe even enjoy champagne and chocolates while in the air.

ACCOMMODATIONS

If you prefer smaller and more personal accommodations, stay at **Rosedale B&B** (377 Lovedale Rd., Lovedale, tel. 02/4990-9537, http://rosedalebnb.com.au, from $150 weekdays, $250 weekends), a family B&B with just three rooms. Enjoy their beautiful gardens, the book and DVD library, and the substantial breakfast.

To get away from it all, why not stay in a cottage by a billabong (watering hole) or even in the trees? The lovingly decorated cottages at **Billabong Moon** (393 Hermitage Rd., Pokolbin, tel. 02/6574-7260, www.billabongmoon.com.au, cottages from $230) are set among large wood- and grassland areas frequented by kangaroos. They even come with breakfast provisions, although you'll have to do the cooking yourself in your own kitchen.

Peppers Guest House (Ekerts Rd., Pokolbin, tel. 02/4993-8999, www.peppers.com.au, rooms from $179 including full buffet breakfast, homestead from $790) offers beautifully appointed rooms in an elegant country-heritage-style house nestled among the vineyards. You can stay in the main house or, if traveling in a group, share the homestead, a separate house that sleeps up to 11 guests and feels like a step back in time. You can even hold your own dinner party—with help from the staff.

Right by the Hunter Valley Gardens and the local golf course, **Mercure Resort Hunter Valley Gardens** (2090 Broke Rd., Pokolbin, tel. 02/4998-2000, www.mercurehuntervalley.com.au, from $179) is a superior motel-style accommodation with elegantly furnished modern rooms but a rustic country-style lobby and bar. It also has a pool, spa, and steakhouse restaurant.

A gorgeous luxury boutique stay, **Tower Lodge** (6 Halls Rd., Pokolbin, tel. 02/4998-4900, www.towerestatewines.com, from $490, two-night minimum stay) looks a little like a convent, with stone floors and columns outside in the secluded courtyard, yet inside it is comfort and coziness all the way. Spacious rooms come with round-the-clock room service and the feeling of being pampered throughout. It's perfect for an indulgent adult weekend.

FOOD

Whether you're sitting on an outdoor terrace overlooking the valley, winery, and lake, or inside next to a roaring fire, dining at **Chez Pok** (Peppers Guest House, Ekerts Rd., Pokolbin, tel. 02/4998-8999, www.peppers.com.au, breakfast Mon.-Fri. 7am-10am and Sat.-Sun. 7:30am-10:30am, lunch Fri.-Sun. 12:30pm-3pm, dinner daily 6:30pm-9:30pm, dinner mains $35) is a treat, especially considering that Chez Pok has a longstanding association with the region; roughly translated it means "among the Pokolbin people." A small but choice menu offers regional ingredients and is inspired by the French chef.

Cafe Enzo (1 Broke Rd., Pokolbin, tel. 02/4998-7233, www.enzohuntervalley.com.au, daily 9am-5pm, breakfast $20, lunch $27) is a rustic and easy-going yet stylish place, where you can sit in the courtyard at wooden tables and enjoy a breakfast or lunch of common staples made fancier: the fish and chips is beer-battered John Dory, the burger is wagyu with beetroot, and the tiger prawns come with shaved parmesan.

Being part of a winery, much of the Bimbadgen Estate's wine is incorporated into the food at **Esca Bimbadgen** (Bimbadgen Estate, 790 McDonalds Rd., Pokolbin, tel. 02/4998-4666, www.bimbadgen.com.au, lunch daily from noon, dinner Wed.-Sat. from 6pm, tasting plates $38) in the form of syrups, caramels, sauces, and, of course, in the accompanying wine list. The setting is sensational, on a hill above the valley, and the tasting plates offer a selection of choice modern Australian cuisine with matched wines.

If you find yourself fancying a beer among all that wine, head to the **Matilda Bay Brewhouse Hunter Valley** (Hunter Valley Resort, Hermitage Rd., Pokolbin, tel. 02/4998-7777, ext. 249, www.hunterresort.com.au/beer-table, daily noon-4pm and 6pm-9pm, bar food $20) and sample some local brews while enjoying some bar snacks in relaxed surroundings. There are no white tablecloths, but there is plenty of music, and even a pool table.

You'll find great food in an unusual indoor garden setting at **The Cellar Restaurant** (Hunter Valley Gardens, 2090 Broke Rd., Pokolbin, tel. 02/4998-7584, www.the-cellar-restaurant.com.au, Mon.-Sat. noon-3pm and 6:30pm-9pm, mains $39, "morsels" $5.50 each). You can dine on great mains, such as deboned spatchcock (a poussin chicken favored in Australia) with Italian sausage; share several "morsels" (the zucchini flowers, meatballs, and calamari are great); or enjoy a charcuterie plate. It's a nice varied menu.

INFORMATION AND SERVICES

The Hunter Valley Wine Country Tourism Centre (455 Wine Country Dr., Pokolbin, tel. 02/4990-0900, www.winecountry.com.au, Mon.-Sat. 9am-5pm, Sun. 9am-4pm) can tell you about all the wineries and restaurants, book accommodations, and get you tickets to local events.

There is also a Hunter Valley iPhone and iPad app, which is free and gives up-to-date information on events, restaurants, accommodations, and everything wine-related. Pick up the annual *Hunter Valley Visitors Guide* from any tourism information bureau in the region—it comes with an excellent touring map in the back.

GETTING THERE AND AROUND

If you are driving, allow a comfortable two hours for your drive. Leave Sydney's CBD via Sydney Harbour Bridge heading north, and follow the Pacific Highway toward Hornsby. Before Hornsby, at Wahroonga, take National Highway 1 (F3 Freeway) north toward Newcastle. After 100 kilometers, around one hour's driving, exit at the Cessnock/Hunter

Valley Vineyards exit sign. Follow the signs to Cessnock/Vineyards. On the way back you could take the scenic route: Head along Tourist Route T33 through Wollombi and the mountains before returning to the National Highway 1 (F3 Freeway) heading south to Sydney.

If you are not driving, there are several day trips up to the Hunter Valley. **Hunter Valley Wine Tasting Tours** (tel. 02/9357-5511, www.huntervalleywinetastingtours.com.au, pickup from hotel around 7am, return 6:30pm, from $100) offers a number of tours, all in smaller 14-seater buses, with stops for coffee, along with taster sessions at five wineries, a cheese shop, and a local chocolate manufacturer, with optional lunches. **AAT Kings** (tel. 1300/228-546, www.aatkings.com.au, depart 8am, return around 7pm, adult $165, child $85) offers a day tour that includes not only visits to a handful of wineries, but also lunch, a taster session at the local beer brewery, and a stop at the famous Hunter Valley Gardens.

MOON SPOTLIGHT SYDNEY
Avalon Travel
a member of the Perseus Books Group
1700 Fourth Street
Berkeley, CA 94710, USA
www.moon.com

Editor and Series Manager: Kathryn Ettinger
Copy Editor: Deana Shields
Graphics Coordinator: Darren Alessi
Production Coordinator: Darren Alessi
Cover Design: Faceout Studios, Charles Brock
Moon Logo: Tim McGrath
Map Editor: Kat Bennett
Cartographer: Stephanie Poulain

ISBN-13: 978-1-61238-918-9

Text © 2015 by Ulrike Lemmin-Woolfrey.
Maps © 2015 by Avalon Travel.
All rights reserved.

Some photos and illustrations are used by permission and are the property of the original copyright owners.

Front cover photo: Sydney Opera House ID 19063995 © Mikeofthethomas | Dreamstime.com
Title page photo: Sydney Harbour Bridge © Anthony Ngo/123rf.com
All photos © Ulrike Lemmin-Woolfrey except page 51 © chaiwat leelakajonkij/123rf.com; page 53 © Rita Melville/123rf.com; page 54 © Heewon Seo/123rf.com; page 55 © rorem/123rf.com; page 63 © Anthony Ngo/123rf.com; page 72 © Thorsten Rust/123rf.com

Printed in the United States

Moon Spotlights and the Moon logo are the property of Avalon Travel. All other marks and logos depicted are the property of the original owners. All rights reserved. No part of this book may be translated or reproduced in any form, except brief extracts by a reviewer for the purpose of a review, without written permission of the copyright owner.

All recommendations, including those for sights, activities, hotels, restaurants, and shops, are based on each author's individual judgment. We do not accept payment for inclusion in our travel guides, and our authors don't accept free goods or services in exchange for positive coverage.

Although every effort was made to ensure that the information was correct at the time of going to press, the author and publisher do not assume and hereby disclaim any liability to any party for any loss or damage caused by errors, omissions, or any potential travel disruption due to labor or financial difficulty, whether such errors or omissions result from negligence, accident, or any other cause.

ABOUT THE AUTHOR

Ulrike Lemmin-Woolfrey

Originally from Hamburg, Germany, Ulrike Lemmin-Woolfrey has lived on three continents and in six countries, including the United Kingdom, Qatar, Oman, and the United Arab Emirates. When her husband relocated to Melbourne, Ulrike found herself packing her bags and heading to the "land down under." Since then, she has made it her mission to see and experience as much as possible of her newly adopted country.

In Sydney, she enjoys immersing herself in the history of the old beautiful buildings and walking the magical Bondi to Coogee coastal path. She has also been known to sit in the Taronga Zoo's petting area to get some one-on-one time with the cuddly critters.

A freelance writer specializing in travel, expat issues, and lifestyle, Ulrike is also the author of *Moon Living Abroad in Australia*. She currently lives in Melbourne.

CPSIA information can be obtained at www.ICGtesting.com
Printed in the USA
LVOW02s1042010315

428470LV00001B/1/P